I Heard It On The 806!

JON BOWERS

I Heard It On The 806!

Published by Kindle Direct Publishing

Printed in the United States of America

ISBN-13: 9781090530301

With deep gratitude...

I wish to thank the many brothers and sisters in Christ Jesus who have helped make this book possible. If I tried to list everyone, it would take another chapter. So to all of the pastors, leaders, churches, each and every member of the Alliance, Christ's Center church and everyone in it, and numerous Ywammers... I am so thankful for all that you have done. What a blessing it has been to co-labor with each of you!

Special honor and thanks go to Jason Hague, his masterful ability to write and communicate were pivotal in capturing my story.

I want to express my gratitude to Nathan R. Sewell, who helped me navigate the whole publishing process. It was smooth due to his knowledge and expertise.

Thanks also to Jerry Dame for his skilled painting of my life-changing moment on the 806. Never has a tractor or an Oregon hayfield looked so good!

Another blessing was Mary Brock who assisted with editing and the coordination of this project. She helped push it across the finish line.

Most of all, I am grateful for my dear wife, Lynna Gay and my precious children, Kim, Todd, and Ryan for standing with me through it all.

To God be the glory.

Now and then, you meet individuals that are quite simply larger than life—people who seem to have lived several lifetimes in a relatively short time, whose adventures in life seem to rival the most popular series on Netflix. I have one such individual for you right here—whose writings are not for your entertainment but rather for your inspiration. His name is Jon Bowers.

I was pleased to meet the Bowers family more than 20 years ago. I came from Harlem, New York, to spend time at their farmhouse in Junction City, Oregon. It was like spending time with Jimmy Stewart and his family in the film "It's a Wonderful Life," they were just as friendly and warm. However, spending time with their congregation—the wild bunch at Christ's Center church was like taking a trip around the world in 80 days.

We traveled from Guatemala to Nicaragua, Cuba, India, Aruba, Russia, Azerbaijan, with the Cowboy church, the Native American church from Oklahoma and, our grand fellowships in Harlem, New York. In these travels, we have seen the hand of God move mightily.

Jon Bower's story is one of high adventure and great persecution where it was just him and his God with a devoted wife praying him through torturous events. In those times of great despair, he would emerge with a look of determination, quickly followed by that famous Jon Bower's half-smile, with another victory intact to bless the body of Christ.

This story is one that will challenge you beyond your comfort zone. It is a book for every believer in the body of Christ. It will uplift, and it will launch dreams. It has been my privilege to have been a part of the journey. I have no doubt that you will be blessed.

Bishop Dr. Carlton T. Brown

Bethel Gospel Assembly, Inc.

Harlem, NY

On September 17, 1996, I drove into Junction City, Oregon. A town I had never hear of. A place I didn't intend to be. To hear a man I had never met. That man was Jon Bowers. Behind that voice was a man who showed me how to love life, love family, love people, and love the work of ministry, and the power of God.

Pursuing God is Jon's great adventure. In this book, you will read about Jon's life. He clearly does not have the objective to arrive at death's door safely. As a matter of fact, his leadership searches for the road less traveled, yet it is cleared by God. Whether you have witnessed the miraculous healings, or his faith for the nations, or his love and investment in the lives of broken and discarded pastors like I was, Jon made it all an adventure pursuing the glory of God.

What I know about this godly man, many more need to know. This book will tell you. It is just a glimpse of what many have seen first-hand. Reading it will inspire you. Your faith level will increase. Your comfort zone will crash! And the Spirit of God in you will bid you to "Come and see." Take up this story and read, and let the passion of this man infect you—for your good, and God's glory!

In His Grip,

Tyrone P. Jones
Lead Pastor
Church for The City
Yuma, AZ

CONTENTS

Chapter 1: The Planting

"Mr. Bowers, do you have your house in order?"

Even in my overwhelmed state, I understood the doctor's implication. This was quadruple bypass surgery. There were no guarantees.

I nodded to him from my bed as the monitor beeped somewhere above me to the rhythm of my damaged heart. My house was indeed in order. Of this I was confident. My wife and children knew how much I loved them. I was not perfect, but I had shown Jesus to my family and my congregation. If I died on that operating table, I would be in the presence of Christ Himself. Not too shabby. But Lynna Gay, my dear wife of thirty-one years would have to go on alone.

The doctor stepped out of the room and for the moment, I was alone.

"God, I have a question to ask. I know time is short."

I was only forty-nine years old, but I had lived a rich forty-nine years. I married my best friend. We had three amazing children who were starting their own families and their own legacies. And for the past fifteen years, we had, as a family, ridden on a more thrilling Holy Spirit roller coaster than I could have ever dreamed existed. We had witnessed electric days of revival. We had fostered a fierce love for men's souls, seeing hundreds and hundreds of conversions. The supernatural had become routine. What more could a pastor ever ask for?

There were so many memories and so many miracles. I was satisfied with my life. I was confident that even if open-heart surgery couldn't save me, I had at least been faithful.

"Tell me Lord, how many talents have I used?"

My question referenced the story Jesus told of a wealthy businessman who gave his servants sums of money—talents, as they were called in the day—and left for a year, expecting them to invest. They did so with varying degrees of success, but only one servant invested all he had been given. He had used all ten of his talents, and the master rewarded him upon his return.

I wasn't so proud to think I had used all ten of my talents, assuming I had been given ten in the first place, but I thought seventy percent was a fair estimate.

"How many, Lord? I'm thinking I've invested seven or eight. That's not so bad, is it?"

Over the years, I had learned to listen when I pray, and God would answer. Sometimes His voice crashed into my heart like a mighty wave slamming into the cliffs of the Oregon coast. Other times, He spoke in whispers like spring rains over the Willamette Valley. That night, in my hospital bed, His answer was soft, but firm.

"You've used only three talents."

I blinked. Three? How was that even possible?

"Lord," I said. "I've given you everything. I've listened. I've obeyed. We've done big things together."

"You were afraid, Jon," God said. "So many times, you pulled back out of fear. There was so much more for you."

Three talents. How could it have only been three talents? I cringed and closed my eyes. My mind returned to a time more than twenty years earlier. The first time a heart attack interrupted my entire world.

***

The Bowers clan was a farming family. Our love for the Oregon soil grew inside us. My grandfather farmed broad, flat fields in the small community of Harrisburg, fifteen miles north of Eugene. To the east stood the towering green Coburg hills, marked by a distinct saddleback shape at their peak. For a flatlander, these hills looked like mountains. But on a cloudless day, when the jagged white peaks of the Cascade Range shows around and through them, it is clear these hills are merely toes of greater giants.

To the west, a softer line of green hills rose out of the ground—the coastal range, the gateway to the spectacular landscapes of Oregon's rugged shoreline. One of the finest perks of growing up in Oregon was the knowledge that a three hour car ride in any direction would land you on completely a different world: a rocky beach, a mountain waterfall, a desert full of mystery.

The outdoors was our playground. My brothers and I grew up swimming in the crisp waters of the Willamette River, hunting pheasants on the prairies, and playing every sport imaginable, even during the tiresome seasons of endless rain.

There were no strangers in our small community and not many secrets either. Everyone went to school together, to church together and to football games together on Friday night. Our phones were on a party line, which meant that at any moment, the town gossip might be listening in on our evening plans.

My parents were active in the community, and faithful in the local Christian church, a conservative, upstanding congregation. During the days of their courtship, Mom had insisted that Dad accept Christ or else she wouldn't marry him. Thankfully, he did, and together, they taught us to live right, work hard, and love God.

All nine of my cousins lived within a mile of our home, and their parents farmed just like my father. It was a family enterprise. Dad had dropped out of school in the eighth grade to help in the fields, and his brothers had done the same. Now, all the aunts and uncles were working the ground just like Grandpa knew they would. My dad grew peppermint and grass seed, sweet corn and hazelnuts, and he made a fine living doing it.

Given the family tradition, there was no question in anyone's mind that I, and my brothers would follow in our father's footsteps. We would marry well, live in Harrisburg, and till the Oregon soil for the rest of our lives. It was simple predestination.

When I fell in love with a local girl from the nearby community of Norton, it looked even more inevitable. Lynna Gay's family was as rooted to the soil as mine was. The closer we became, the more certain our future appeared.

But during our high school courtship, something else began to burn inside my heart—a different kind of farming. Getting crops to grow was one thing. Getting minds and hearts to grow was another. I wanted to grow people. I wanted to teach.

It's hard to say when that desire began, but the sensation is clear to this day, I was addicted to the smell of chalk. The classroom was, to me, a rich place, an exciting place. I wanted to be there. I wanted to explain things. I wanted to see the faces of students light up with the astonishment that only comes with new knowledge.

This might sound like a simple rejection of family norms, but it wasn't. On the contrary, I admired the farming profession and the lifestyle. I even enjoyed the work. But in my bones, I felt the assurance of a different call. Farming was a wonderful part of our heritage, it just wasn't for me.

This awakening carried with it a dull, sickening ache in the pit of my stomach. I knew what the family would say. It would be a shock that felt like betrayal. But by the time I graduated high school in 1961, my desire had at last overwhelmed my fears. I announced my intention to go to college and study the art of education.

The result was predictable, but nonetheless painful.

"You're a fool!" Grandpa Bowers lashed. "All these years, we've cared for you and made a place for you. Now you want to go and throw it all away in college? You'll never be able to make a living." Then, he gave a prediction that would haunt me for some time. "You'll be back."

My family remained cordial with me, but our relationship was, without question, strained.

Lynna Gay stuck with me through it all, however, and in the fall of 1963, roughly halfway into my four years at Southern Oregon State College, we were married.

When I graduated, I took a job at Kennedy Jr. High back in Eugene. It was a fine time for my budding family. We had our first child, our daughter Kim, and a few years later, Todd came along. We were a happy, active foursome, full of laughter and adventure.

On a professional level, teaching was everything I hoped it would be. In the classroom, I taught history, sociology, and speech, and after school I would coach basketball. But soon, something else began to happen which I had not expected. When the principal didn't know how to deal with troubled students, he would often seek me out. He saw I had a way with them, and he began to count on me to talk them down. Even when I was in the middle of a lecture, my boss would pull in the school librarian to cover my class while I worked with a student. Soon, the principal moved the librarian's office next to my classroom just to make it easier.

What most people did not know was that I was openly sharing Jesus with these kids when I sat with them. Even in the 1960's, that was against the rules, but I didn't care. They needed something more than strict discipline. They needed the love of Christ, and I was determined to give it to them. In a short time, my position had grown from being a mere teaching job to a teaching *ministry*, and it felt like destiny.

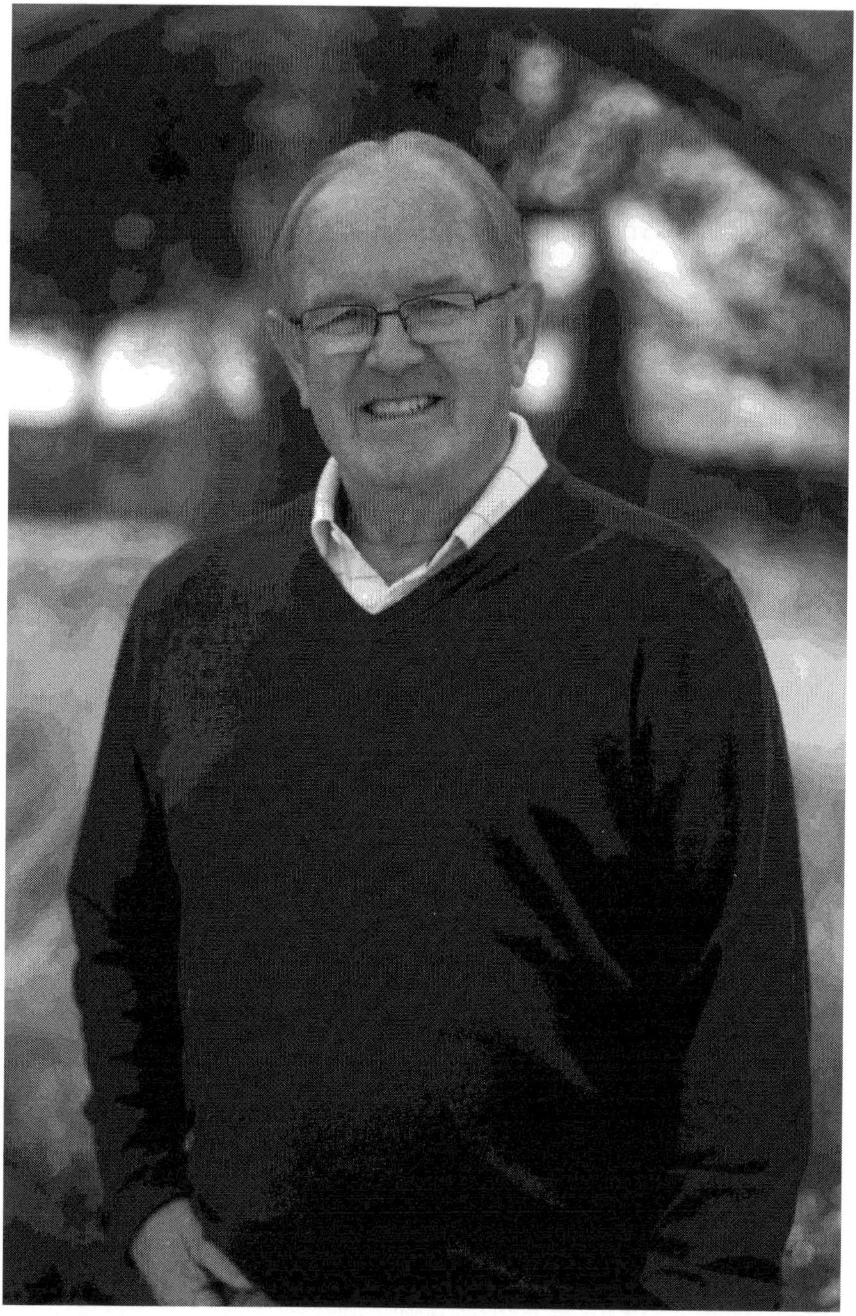

Jon Bowers

The only problem was the pay. I was only bringing in $320 per month. That was a small sum to support a family on even in that day, and I knew I could make many times that much on the farm. In the back of my mind, my grandfather's words still haunted me.

But I wasn't about to give up. I decided to go back to school to earn my master's degree. That way, I could continue teaching, but also work in administration. The pay would be better, and there would be more opportunities to influence teachers and students for the Lord. I was confident in this plan. It made sense, and it capitalized on my gifting.

Then, in 1970, during my final semester of grad school, the phone rang. It was my mom. Dad had just suffered a heart attack, and the family needed me to come home.

I was devastated. Dad would recover, they said, but my dreams were put on hold. The family was farming more than 1200 acres of mint, and without dad it was an overwhelming task. I knew the business. I was a competent farmer, fully capable of helping to expand the operation. But the smell of chalk was all gone and Grandpa Bowers was proven right.

We moved back into the Harrisburg area, dejected but resigned to our fate. Over the first year, the farm did well. Oregon is famous for its mint crop, and our mint oil was second to none. We could make it so well and at such high volumes that buyers came calling from all over the world, and before long, we had become our own brokers, flying ourselves to Europe and Japan to meet with new buyers personally. Business was booming.

The success of the farm was little consolation to me, however. I didn't care how much money I was making, provided I could support my family. All I wanted was to finish my degree and go back to school to do what I was made to do. But I was stuck, and I was angry with God. He had been the One, after all, who made the desire to teach burn inside me. He gave me success but then, it seemed, pulled it all away from me. I felt so lost.

It all came to a head one clear spring morning while I plowed a field of sandy loam. I was driving a red 806 International Tractor—the classic kind with two small wheels on the front and two giant ones in the back. Behind me, the four-bottom plow turned over the soil, sending up clouds of dust that could be seen for miles. I carried with me a portable radio, tuned to a Christian station broadcasting from Eugene. A popular preacher of the day, Jimmy Swaggart, was delivering a heartfelt message.

"There's someone out there right now who's upset with God," he said as he drew his talk to a close.

"You're complaining to God right now about His timing." At these words, I sat up a little straighter. "If that's you, stop what you're doing right now and listen."

He had my attention now. It seemed a silly thing to do, but I did it anyway. I stopped the tractor and turned off the engine.

For the next several minutes, the preacher held me spellbound. I couldn't speak. I couldn't move. Every word from his mouth was for me. I just knew it.

"You need to trust the Holy Spirit," the man concluded.

And right then, I knew my problem. The preacher had exposed me with that sentence. I didn't have the Holy Spirit, so how could I trust Him? In my church, the Holy Spirit was an unwelcome topic, an awkward intruder. We believed in God the Father, and we trusted His Son for our salvation, but we were more than a little leery of that Spirit of His.

"The Holy Spirit isn't a thing, He's a Person!" Swaggart insisted. "And He wants you to succeed and thrive. Do you know Him? Do you have the Holy Spirit?"

I heard it on the 806. I knew I had to respond.

I sank to my knees, feeling that all the struggles that had warred inside my chest were merely symptoms of this great lack. I wanted everything God had for me. I wanted His Spirit inside me. And I asked Him to fill me.

And there, in that field of replanting, God plowed my heart. He heard my prayer.

This book is the story of how He responded to that prayer. I'm warning you now, it's a wild story, a story far too big for me. It's a story of risk, of danger, and of trust. Some of it will sound far-fetched, and that's okay. As I wrote all this down, it sounded far-fetched to me, too. If I hadn't lived it, I might not have believed it myself. I'm just a farmer from a small town in Oregon, after all. Who was I to start a ministry that God would set on fire? Who was I to travel across the globe, or to meet such strange and wonderful brothers along the way? Who was I to inherit nations, to stand before kings, and to help turn a prison on its head from the inside?

I'm a simple man, that's all. A man who God filled to stretching; a man who had to learn and relearn and relearn again what the old hymn says:

When we walk with the Lord in the light of His Word,
What a glory He sheds on our way!
While we do His good will, He abides with us still,
And with all who will trust and obey.

I heard it on the 806. And it is my prayer that you hear His call, wherever you are. You don't have to be a person of means or of influence. You don't have to be a theologian like the Apostle Paul, or a great musician like Keith Green. You don't even have to have all your stuff together. All you have to do is turn off your own tractor and heed his call. All you have to do is trust and obey.

The 806

Chapter 2: The Breaking

The first gift that came was love. After my prayer in the field, I began to care about people's souls in a way I never had before, and that gave me a purpose even in my holding pattern. When people talk about the gifts of the Holy Spirit, they talk about the messy part—tongues, healings, wonders—and I was about to experience all of that. But before those things came, the love of the Spirit of God met my heart in a surprising way.

I was teaching Sunday school at my church in Harrisburg, which was part of the Disciples of Christ Denomination. My church didn't believe much in the Holy Spirit. Oh, we said we did, but we didn't really. Not in any way that mattered, anyway. Doctrinally, we were cessationists. We believed that the Spirit's gifts had ceased long ago. But now, I knew my church's strict stance couldn't be true, because of the love. My heart had already expanded, and I knew more was coming.

That change in me, it seemed, was apparent. People began flocking in early to hear me teach. They could sense I was different, and I really was. I had a newfound affection for people's souls. I cared for them, and I wanted them to meet God in all His fullness.

One morning, Noel Campbell came to hear me teach. Noel was a friend of mine and a man I had a profound respect for. He was an elder at Eugene Faith Center, a charismatic congregation that was well known throughout the community. But in my church, charismatic churches were treated with theological scorn.

Noel sat and listened to my message in its entirety. Technically, I was supposed to be teaching out of our denomination's Sunday school manual for the adult class, a publication called The Quarterly. It was a strict Sunday-by-Sunday lesson plan. And above all things, it was safe.

I didn't like The Quarterly. The Holy Spirit didn't seem to be in there much, and I wanted to talk about Him, the One who was enlarging my heart. So I opened up the book of Acts and talked about Pentecost. I talked about the miraculous deeds of the apostles. I talked about how the Spirit infused Peter and Paul, and how we still need Him today.

Noel sat quietly, smiling to himself. At the end of the session, he pulled me aside and took me into his confidence.

"Jon, I want to introduce you to my pastor, Roy Hicks, Jr."

I winced at the name. I knew of Roy Hicks, Jr. We all did. He was a firebrand. A loose cannon. Things happened in his church that weren't supposed to happen. He was just the type of man my heart was already burning to see. But I was timid.

"No way. I've heard of Roy Hicks, Jr. He's a Looney Tune!"

Noel gave a knowing smile. "No, he's not! You need to come and see."

Those words were a calm challenge, and they mirrored Jesus' own response to Peter and Andrew when they first met Him. Jesus captivated those two would-be disciples, in the same way I was intrigued by the Holy Spirit. They wanted more than to just observe him. They wanted to follow Him. So they asked Him where He was staying.

"Come and see," He told them.

So I went. I began by sneaking into the services, keeping my head down. The music was loud, and the preaching was in your face, and the services were alive. Pastor Roy would preach not only about the love of the Holy Spirit, but also of His power. And then, things would happen that never happened at my church.

People got saved. They spoke in strange languages that they had never been taught. Some people were healed of sicknesses and diseases right there in the sanctuary. Everywhere I looked, there was evidence of the mysterious power of the Holy Spirit whom I had only just met.

It was not a clean, orderly sight. It was messy, and sometimes it was even unnerving. But the Holy Spirit was there. I could feel Him there. And I was thoroughly hooked on His presence.

Sometimes, people from town would see me at those services. They would give me questioning looks. They knew. They knew what my denomination would think about me being there. I knew it too.

"What are you doing here, Jon?" They would ask with a raised eyebrow.

All I could do was shrug. "I can't explain it, but I like what I see."

Roy Hicks Jr. was a bold preacher, and his boldness did not let up when I had coffee with him. He knew I was hungry. I told him as much. I told him all about my prayer by the tractor and about Sunday school and how I wanted to lead people into all God had for them.

"It won't work, Jon," he said. "Not yet. You need the power of the Holy Spirit." I agreed to that, at least in theory. Sure, I had just opened my heart to the Holy Spirit, but Roy was suggesting that if I wanted to make a big impact for God's kingdom, I needed His power, too. All of those strange happenings in Roy's church didn't occur by accident. No, those were the gifts of the Spirit in action, given for the purpose of ministry to others. I knew it was true. I needed the gifts of the Spirit. There was only one problem.

"Lord," I complained later on in prayer, "I want all you have for me. I really do. But I don't want to…you know…be weird!"

There it was in all its plain ugliness. It was fear of man. I didn't want to look stupid. I had seen the excesses, and they embarrassed me: people flopping all over a stage, barking like dogs, making everybody cringe. I didn't want to be associated with those guys. Better to play it safe, I thought. Better to keep the Holy Spirit in a vault where He could be my personal Encourager. My nice little pet God.

I heard Him respond gently to my fearful heart. "Was Jesus weird?"

I thought about the question. I wouldn't call Jesus normal, but He wasn't weird, either. Not in the way I was thinking. Weird people drove others away. Jesus drew people *to* Himself, and to the Father. Why, then, would the Spirit of God be any different?

The implication was clear. The Holy Spirit knew what He was doing. If I let Him have His way in my heart, He would empower me to actually do the things God called me to. He would draw people *to* the Father, not away. In short, I could trust Him. But it might not be easy. He would stretch me.

It was time to let go of my pride. The Holy Spirit was bigger than me, and He wanted out of the vault. "Fine, Lord." I told Him one afternoon while driving to the local Dairy Mart. "Holy Spirit, I won't let shame rule me. I'm embracing everything you have."

The next moment, I found myself speaking in a language I had never learned. It was a language of prayer intended for the Holy Spirit alone. I knew what it was right away, the gift of tongues. I started to sing in that prayer language, and my heart swelled two sizes. It was as if I was floating on a river of pure peace.

When I got home, I tried to play it cool, but I failed miserably. Lynna Gay noticed something was different. "What happened to you?" she asked, and for a moment, I almost didn't tell her. I was too embarrassed. But then I remembered the vault. "I gave you a gift, Jon." the Lord seemed to say. "Don't be ashamed of it."

"Honey, I don't want to shock you," I began, "but I was singing in tongues on the way home."

I braced myself for a skeptical reaction, but my wife merely grinned and said, "Can you show me?" I sighed in relief. Soon, she received the same gift.

We both knew we had stepped over a line. On this side, there was excitement and life and a whole new world of possibilities. On the other side were my church and my family. A confrontation was inevitable.

My Sunday school class continued to grow. We met in a classroom an hour before service, and people were flocking to it. After my encounter with the Holy Spirit, I was teaching with both affection and power. The combination was palpable. In a matter of weeks, we were packed out. The class was spilling out into the hallway, and they were still coming. So I made what I thought was an innocuous logistical decision.

"Let's go out in the auditorium," I told them. We went.

That morning, with more than a hundred listeners, I spoke about the ways of the Holy Spirit. I told them of His gifts and His power, and I didn't hold back. In the middle of the message, one lady jumped to her feet and exclaimed, "My God, I'm not saved! I need to receive Jesus right now!"

At that, another lady called out, "I'm not saved, either!" These were not women who had never heard the gospel before. They were part of the church, but they realized that had never surrendered their lives to Christ or trusted in His Spirit. I prayed with them right then and there, and they received the salvation of Jesus Christ.

It went on like that for weeks. The crowd swelled to more than one hundred twenty, and more people received Christ. For some people, that class became the main event on a Sunday. They would come to Sunday school, and then they would go on home and skip the main service. That's when I got the call from the pastor.

"We need to talk."

I should have seen it coming. Indeed, I knew my newfound convictions would eventually collide with my church's theology, but I didn't expect it to happen so soon, or in such a personal way.

I sat in his office and he began. "Jon, you had no authority to use the sanctuary for your class. That was wrong." I searched his face. He was serious.

"And I don't like what you're doing in that class. You're getting people worked up and emotional. It's not right. And you shouldn't be leading them to Jesus in that class."

I was utterly taken aback. "You don't want me to lead people to the Lord?"

"That's for the main service!" he said.

In short, he wanted his safe class back. He wanted a safe lecture from the Quarterly where people learned just the right lessons to make them good Disciples of Christ. I, of course, had no interest in giving him that. But he was the pastor. I was just a Sunday school teacher. I hadn't been trying to rock the boat in the first place, and I didn't want to start a revolt now. I was just trying to be faithful to what God was teaching me.

I suppose I must have been a particularly difficult case for the pastor. After all, I had grown up in that church. My brother was currently the head elder, and my parents were still worshipping there, stalwart as ever and woven into the fabric of the community. We were all family. If I had been anyone else, they probably wouldn't have needed outside confirmation that I was unfit to lead. But that's exactly what they sought.

They found it in a professor at Northwest Christian College in Eugene. He was obviously a brilliant man who they respected. They called him in, told him their view of the situation, and asked for his opinion on how to deal with me.

I didn't know about any of it—their outsourcing or the professor's conclusion—until one afternoon when I was working hard at the mint distillery. That's when Merril Rush came to see me. I had known Merril my whole life. He was a dear and kind man. He had been an elder for as long as I could remember, and his wife was my Sunday school teacher as a kid. I had a profound respect for both of them.

Merril got out of his truck and leaned against my pickup, carefully searching for the right words. I was already on edge. I knew something was up.

"Jon, I want you to know that the elders are very concerned about you."

"Okay."

"We think…we think you're either demon possessed or are having a nervous breakdown."

I froze. I couldn't have responded even if I tried. How could I? What could I possibly say? These men…they were my brothers. This man himself was like an uncle. I was devastated.

We both sat there, saying nothing. Finally, Merril got back in his truck, having delivered his message, and drove away.

Of course, the elders called a meeting. It would be a follow-up to what the pastor had already discussed with me, but it would be more than that. It would hurt far more.

They were assembled like a jury who had already made up their minds before the trial began. I was guilty. I could see it in their faces. Merril, my friend Bill Morris, and even Jim, my own dear brother. Face after face looked down on me with a mix of sadness and resolution.

They rehashed the concerns the pastor had. I was not teaching the right things the right ways in the right place. I was out of line. I was way out of line.

I listened to them, taking it all in, fully aware now of where this was going.

"Jon, let me ask you a question. Do you speak in tongues?"

The room grew quiet. In this setting, that was an accusation, not a question. I sat for a moment, thinking of how to answer it.

And again, I remembered what the Holy Spirit had whispered to me on the way to Dairy Mart. "Don't be ashamed of Me."

I cleared my throat and answered them. "Yes. Yes, I speak in tongues."

One of the elders started pounding the table saying, "I knew it! I knew it!" and the room erupted in disgust. The gift of tongues ended in the book of Acts. It was pure foolishness. No, it was worse than that. It was the devil's work. It was more evidence of their conclusion. Jon Bowers was either demon possessed or having a nervous breakdown.

I didn't try very hard to defend myself. I was only trying to teach and live according to what I saw in scripture. This is what I saw. God was an active God, and He did things—unexpected things—through His Spirit. Who was I to resist His work in the church? Or in myself?

But none of that went over with anyone. In their eyes, I was guilty of something more than heresy against my denomination. I had betrayed my church.

There was only one man who cast any kind of doubt on their decision. Bill Morris, my friend and fellow businessman. He was visibly torn.

"I don't know guys," he said. "What if he's right?"

That question threw the meeting into further disgust. "What if he's right? Are you kidding me?"

If I had been hoping my brother Jim would rescue me, I soon realized it wasn't going to happen. I saw the look on his face. It was shame.

"Listen, I understand what you all are saying," I said at last. "It's obvious that I no longer have a place here, so I'm going to resign."

The meeting was over, as was my membership at Harrisburg Christian Church.

Over the next several weeks, things got ugly. Many of my friends were furious with the eldership. They got angry and lashed out at the church. Then, the eldership lashed back. Accusations were made that should not have been. Relationships broke down. And in the end of it all, Lynna Gay and I were on the outside looking in. We didn't just lose our church, we lost our entire community.

It was a shocking blow, and a confusing one. But the worst part of it was that my parents sided with the elders. In their mind, I had rocked the boat. I had turned against my own. I had morphed into something else—something foreign—and they were ashamed.

Mother was a peacemaker at heart, so she at least reached out to us. Dad though? Not him. He was so angry and embarrassed that for the next three years, he refused to associate with me. He wouldn't even speak to me on the telephone. My wife and I were utterly devastated.

I talked with Pastor Roy about all of it. He was a friend now, and I respected his opinion on pretty much everything. My chief concern was the broken relationships. I didn't want them to stay broken. I knew even then that I could fix everything by simply changing my tune and going back to Harrisburg Christian with hat in hand. I could agree to abide by the rules and return to the doctrines of the church. But that would have meant turning my back on the Holy Spirit, and there was no way I could do that. I had seen too much.

"Jon, what you need to do is treat them all as if they already agree with you."

It was a simple strategy, which, at its base required that I refuse to hold a grudge. In that way, it was a brutal thing to advise. Resentment was my right, wasn't it? Hadn't I only done what God had told me to do? Hadn't they been the ones to reject me?

But those feelings soon melted away. The love of the Holy Spirit was dwelling in my heart now, after all. How could a frozen thing like resentment stand a chance in front of His flame?

Thus, in the midst of the hardest season of our lives, Lynna Gay and I chose to forgive. We chose to trust that God Himself would defend and vindicate us. Soon, He would do that and far more.

Chapter 3: The Beginning

The Lord promised in the book of Isaiah, "When you pass through the waters, I will be with you; and through the rivers, they shall not overwhelm you; when you walk through fire you shall not be burned, and the flame shall not consume you." Lynna Gay and I believed this, and every word of it turned out to be true. Even if we had been completely alone, He would have preserved us.

Fortunately, we didn't have to walk through this season by ourselves. We had brothers and sisters in Christ who not only stuck with us but also championed us. Many of these had been part of our Bible study, and they were getting hooked on the Holy Spirit as well. They weren't about to let a little thing like church expulsion get in the way of what He was doing in their lives. They wanted to keep moving forward in the love for Christ, and in their experiences with His Spirit.

It is worth noting that this type of scenario was not rare in those days. All over the country, the Holy Spirit was showing up in meetings and making a mess of churches. It had been happening since the late 60's. They called it "The Jesus Movement." It started with the hippies. Some churches didn't like that these long-haired weirdos were showing up on Sunday looking for something real. The old guard felt like they were losing control, and they probably were. And that was a good thing.

During that season, new churches were popping up all around the country. Some of them put the lion's share of emphasis on the

Holy Spirit, and many, such as the Vineyard Churches, are still thriving today. Other already established churches saw the movement as a good thing, and they stretched and adapted in order to make a place for healing, tongues, and prophecy. "The real thing."

I wasn't a hippy, but I was undoubtedly part of that large movement now. Jesus was behind it, and His Spirit was beckoning us all forward. We decided to continue with my class. It would be in the form of a Bible study now. We would sing songs of worship, I would teach, and we would let the Holy Spirit do whatever it was He wanted to do.

Of course, we couldn't meet at the church ever again, and we didn't like the idea of doing it on a Sunday morning. So we prayed about it and decided it to host it right on our own property. We didn't have an auditorium or anything like that. What we did have, however, was a barn.

The barn sat next to an open field behind our farmhouse on a back road in Junction City. It was a tall, narrow structure with high rafters, and we filled it with folding metal chairs. Then, we brought lights in. The result did not look very impressive, but people came.

We gathered on Thursday nights and sat inside under the low lights. We prayed hard and sang loud and did our best to ignore the mice running back and forth overhead across the rafters. We disregarded the meager surroundings. All of it was a testament to the quality of our thirsty hearts. This wasn't about church; it was about the Holy Spirit! Who needed a church building? Certainly not Him!

Those were electric nights. I preached with more desperation than ever before. My heart was broken but determined. We all cried out to God together, and He was faithful to show up. The Holy Spirit graced us with the love that comes with His presence.

And soon, it happened. He began pouring out His controversial gifts on us all—tongues, healings, words of prophecy. We didn't understand it all, but we could feel ourselves being changed.

We went on like that for months. One night, a car drove up that we did not recognize, and an elderly gentleman got out. He introduced himself as Harry Dingamin, and he wanted to join us. Far from being a young zealot, Harry was gray haired with a peaceful face and a slow, serious voice. But he had come to be a part of what was happening.

Someone in town, it seemed, had told Harry that there was some Holy Spirit meeting out in the backcountry, and he had decided to go for a drive to find it.

"The Lord told me, Go out to the country and where the light is shining that is where My Spirit will be," he told us.

I've always remembered that answer. He saw the light. It was only a barn light, and yet it was much more. It was the light of God's Spirit. Penetrating. Blinding. This was the beginning of something grand, and I think we could all sense God was on the move.

Roy Hicks was the first to recognize what was probably obvious to everyone but me. "Jon," he said, "You've got a church here."

I hemmed and hawed. It wasn't a church; it was just a Bible study. I didn't have enough formal training to be a pastor. I was a teacher, yes, and a farmer, but I wasn't a pastor.

But he would shake his head and say, "Jon, you are a pastor, and it's time you accept it."

Deep down, I could see the lights, too, and I knew he spoke the truth.

"What would we call the church?" Lynna Gay asked. I didn't know. Neither did I know where we would meet. And there was also that ordination thing. I was still a layman, after all.

Pastor Roy took care of that last concern. He agreed to ordain me under the Foursquare Church banner. I didn't need seminary for that, just a Foursquare pastor to vouch for me that I was anointed of the Lord to preach the gospel.

Then, Noel Campbell said this: “Jon, I think I have a name for you. Christ’s Center, with an apostrophe ’s.”

That made me grimace. An odd name to be sure. But I liked it. I liked the theme. We would not put traditions of men at the center of our worship. If I was going to pastor a church, I needed Jesus to be at the center of all things.

Lynna Gay greeted me when I got home. “Jon, I think I’ve got the name!” she exclaimed.

I didn’t tell her that Noel had already picked a name. Oh well. I could let her down easy. “What is it?” I asked.

“It’s a little odd, but I think we should call it Christ’s Center, with an apostrophe ’s.”

“Praise God,” I laughed.

Those two words have become a central part of my personal lexicon. When God does something unexpected and awesome, I laugh and drag out the words: “Praaaaaise God.” When people would blame me for something I didn’t do and leave the church without warning, I say it quickly with a shrug: “Well, praise God.” Because it doesn’t matter what the situation is. God is always worthy of praise. Whether we are on cloud nine in the heavens, or going through the depths of Sheol, He is always worthy to be praised. That day, I praised Him for His simple confirmation. He was building a church, yes, but He was also building my faith in him.

Unfortunately, the process of growing in faith can be messy. My faith was still young and often raw. Even though I felt I had walked in grace and obedience during this entire transition out of my former church into this new one, I still had a tendency to ignore His voice in other areas. His grace, in the end, would cover those failures. But some of my lapses came at a cost.

The first area was the church leadership. I knew Roy was right about me being a pastor, but I did not want to do it alone. I was still a farmer, after all, and I had a business to run.

So I presented an idea to Pastor Roy. I had a friend in town, Gordon Johnson by name, who had recently returned from mission work abroad. He was, and remains today, a good and a godly man. My proposition was that we could run the church together, Gordon and I. We could co-pastor.

"It won't work, Jon," Roy said. "It won't work."

We went back and forth on it, and deep down in my heart, I knew he was right. I knew what happens in those types of shared leadership situations. It was good and healthy to work in teams, and wisdom certainly comes in many counselors, but ultimately, there needed to be one person who would be responsible to make the call.

Roy just shook his head. And as he did, I knew the Lord was confirming that warning. Nevertheless, I pushed my plan forward, and Gordon and I were ordained as co-pastors of Christ's Center Church. I will tell more of that story later, but suffice it to say if I had listened to the Holy Spirit the first time, I would have saved both Gordon and myself a lot of heartache.

We had our personnel in place, now, and we had adopted the name, but we still had no facility. We had outgrown the barn by then, and I knew if we were to become a "real church," we needed a real building. And I had my eye on one.

Even though I wasn't a teacher anymore, I was still quite involved in the community. I was an elected member of the school board, and I had been appointed chairman of a special committee to sell Central Elementary School in Junction City. It was an aptly named school because it sat right smack dab in the center of the map. The main building contained a handful of large classrooms, administrative offices and a full gymnasium. Next to it was a second building with a large kitchen and cafeteria. There was also a playground area and a small football field out back. The district had now outgrown the facility. As a school, it was pretty small. But as a church, it would be perfect.

The Lord spoke clearly to my heart. "This is where I'm going to house My church." The thought thrilled me. Right away, I decided that I should excuse myself as chairman of the committee. It would be a conflict of interest. Stepping down was an act of faith. I wish I could say my faith was strong all the way through the process, but that would be a lie.

I had an idea to give the school board an offer. My family owned a piece of property on the edge of town that I knew would be attractive to the city. The Jensen Property, we called it, and it was huge—forty acres in all. That was almost fifteen times the size of the property they were selling. I wanted to offer a straight up trade of the properties.

My brothers signed off on the idea, and I figured it would be a no-brainer for the committee. There was a problem in my heart, however, and it was a simple one. I was being utterly disobedient. God had spoken clearly to my heart to make a different offer. We were not to trade properties, we were to bid on the school, and the bid would be small. One hundred thousand dollars.

That's what God spoke. I thought it was crazy. Even in those days, the property was worth far more than that. I thought there was no way they would ever agree to it, so I rejected God's voice and made my own offer.

The property had been advertised for the past six weeks, so I expected a good deal of competition. On the appointed night of the sale, the chairman opened the envelope, and only one bid fell out. My bid. My trade proposal for the Jensen property. They read it aloud, and they said sorry, but no.

I couldn't believe it. There was no logical reason for them to turn down that deal. The Jensen Property was worth far more than the school. And yet, I knew I shouldn't be surprised. It never had been God's plan. He had given me a different strategy, and I had ignored it.

"Are you ready to do it My way, Jon?" He seemed to say.

I sighed, "Yes, Lord. I'm ready."

The school board's refusal turned out to be a great mercy. There were no other bids. So it seemed to me right then that God was offering me a mulligan.

I stood up and said something bold. "Legally you have to give us one more chance for a counter offer since we were the only bid."

The chairman turned to the lawyer in the group, and the man nodded. I was correct, he said.

Here is the funny part—I had no idea what I was talking about. I didn't know that rule actually existed. I just jumped up and said it. The fact that they confirmed it was, in hindsight, definitely a good sign. God was going before us. I had messed up the first time. This time, if I did it right, He was going to come through.

The committee was irritated by the whole situation, but they reluctantly agreed to adjourn and regroup a week later. They set the meeting for the worst possible time, Monday evening during the Monday Night Football game. These were the days when everyone watched Monday Night Football. The committee clearly didn't want anyone to show up.

But I showed up with my prayer team, and we were ready. We met right there in the cafeteria building of the school property. It was a wide, echoing building. Not very inviting.

When it was time, they read the new bid. $100,000 for the entire property.

They room erupted in frustration. The chairman of the board was furious. "What a ridiculous offer! This is a dead issue, Jon," he told me, " and you're wasting our time!"

But they still had to discuss it, so they dismissed us during the deliberations. My team and I stepped outside into the breezeway and started to pray. They were angry inside. We could hear them. I had clearly not made a good impression.

Then, I heard God speak to my heart again. "If they call you back in to argue, tell them they now have to throw in all the classroom furniture and classroom materials for free. That is their punishment for arguing with Me in this."

Soon, the door opened and they called me back in. They were still irate. "Jon, this is the stupidest thing ever!"

I winced. It had happened. But by now, I had nothing to lose. I told them exactly what God had said. So instead of rescinding my ridiculous offer, I told them it now included the desks, the tables and chairs, everything. All $50,000 worth.

Of course, that didn't improve their mood. They told me to go wait outside again. So I did. I started praying with my team like I had before. More yelling inside interrupted our prayers. Shouting and cursing exploded. It might have been intimidating at another time, but we were undaunted. God had spoken. Somehow, His word would carry the day.

When the clerk called me back in to hear their decision, the room had quieted significantly.

We sat down and waited. Then, the chairman spoke.

"While you were out, we had a motion and it was upheld unanimously. Jon Bowers, your bid stands. The building and all the materials therein will be sold for a sum of $100,000."

We rejoiced openly.

The question has been asked many times, "what in the world happened to make them change their minds so quickly?"

One witness told us he could feel a tangible presence in the room. It was as if something—or Someone—came into the midst of all the anger, the ridicule, the cursing, and replaced those emotions with a sort of inexplicable urgency, as if they could not help but hurry up and get the deal done. "It was the darnedest thing I'd ever seen!" He told us.

Soon, we were walking through our new property. We started in the cafeteria, then through the empty halls of the main building, the classrooms stocked with tables and chairs, and finally into the center of the gymnasium that would become our auditorium.

"How are we ever going to fill it?" We asked ourselves. It seemed like an impossibility. We could fill a small barn, but a building like this?

We knew, however, that growing the church wasn't our responsibility. The Lord would build His church as He had promised.

And we knew already that He fulfills His promises. The night with the building committee proved that to us. It became a seminal moment that we continue to look back on with wonder. For there, at the founding of Christ's Center Church, was an absurdity made real by the Holy Spirit. God spoke and God came through. Our house would be a house of miracles.

Chapter 4: The Healing

The first Sunday we met in our building, we lost half our congregation. It seemed the financial burden weighed too heavily on some, and they backed away. But it didn't matter. After only a few months, we were already too big to fit comfortably in the cafeteria, so we moved into the gymnasium. We felt like a real church, now. We were Christ's Center, His church.

The Sunday Services were fun in those days, in part because we didn't know what we were doing. From week to week, we never quite knew what was going to happen.

Despite that fact—or maybe because of it—we grew quickly. Services were exciting. Our worship was terrific. God seemed to bring us excellent musicians with an intense love for the Lord. And I was preaching now with confidence and passion. That drew people too, I think.

Without a doubt, though, the main factor that drew people in was the love for and from the Holy Spirit. He had poured out His affection into our hearts, and it showed. People would visit, and they felt something different. They felt like someone genuinely cared for them. And they would stay.

We still had all those classrooms, though and we didn't know what to do with them until Gordon, my co-pastor, had a mind to start a Christian school. It was an excellent idea. I had maintained my love for teaching and education, after all, and Gordon was a gifted teacher himself. Plus, we were already attracting talented parents and teachers who could jump in and help build it. And of course, we had kids. Lots of kids. My son Ryan had joined us by then, so I had three of my own.

In 1976, just one year after we bought the building, Christ's Center School began, and it quickly became a large part of our community. Many of our congregants joined, as did a whole host of people around the community. Gordon was the principal while I became the athletic director and music director. And we succeeded almost immediately.

All of a sudden, life was hectic. Sometimes when God blesses you—when He answers your prayers for success—it can become a challenge just to keep up. And while that season was exhilarating in many ways, it was still painful. I was still a heretic in the eyes of old friends and even branded a sort of religious madman by my former church.

Meanwhile, my family continued to ignore me. I missed them. I missed my father. The wounds were still fresh. Little did I know, that the Lord was about to do a deep work of healing.

It started with my brother Jim. We were still running the family farm, so we never became complete strangers. We had to talk, though at first, those conversations were only about the family business.

Over time, however, this began to change. His heart softened toward me, and we started to discuss the way his elder board had treated me. I could sense some regret in his voice. We met one day with another of the elders, Kay Smith, and the words finally came out: "what we did was wrong."

Soon, Kay left Harrisburg Christian and started attending Christ's Center. That did not help relationships with the old church, but it warmed my heart.

Then, one Sunday morning, it happened. Jim himself showed up in one of the services. He came marching down the center aisle with his wife Judy and came up to the front.

"I want you all to know," he said to the congregation, "that this is my brother Jon. But from now on, he is also my pastor."

The healing had begun.

Lynna Gay and I were moved by the gesture, and we found it easy to forgive. God had prepared our hearts early on. We really had done our best to put relationship over controversy. So when the controversy finally dried up, we found we didn't have grudges to block those relationships from reforming.

In Jim's case, healing required time and deep conversation. In my father's case, however, it took another health crisis.

Lynna Gay found me running along the road one morning. "Jon, your mom just called," she said out the window of the car. "Your Dad just had another heart attack. He's at home and says he's not going to the hospital. Jon, he wants to see you."

Dad had recovered from his first heart attack years earlier, but he had never gone back to work. That crisis had taken a toll on his body, and he had been on medication for years, seeing a cardiologist on a regular basis. This one, I knew, must be especially serious. The fact that he was calling for me after three years of radio silence meant that the situation must be grim.

I went home, showered up, and in a few minutes, I was standing by my father's bedside with no words.

I cleared my throat and gave a limp greeting. How do you greet anyone in that setting, let alone your own father? "Hey, Dad. What's up?"

"I've had a heart attack, Jon. I'm not going to the hospital. I want…" he looked up at me with earnest eyes. "Jon, I want you to call your elders. I want them to come anoint me with oil and pray for my healing."

I was stunned. I said, "Dad, call your own elders. Why would you want my elders who you don't even agree with?"

He dismissed my question. "Oh son, you know they don't believe in that. I want people who have faith to believe that I can be healed."

It was a startling turnabout and a generous sentiment. Still, I couldn't be sure if this was the crisis talking, or if he really meant it.

"Okay, Dad, but listen. If my elders come over, it won't look the way you want it to look. They will speak in tongues, and they'll cry out to God for your healing. Is that really what you want?"

He did. The severity of the moment trumped all sense of religious decorum. We were past the time for safe, predictable doctrine. What we needed was a miracle. Dad knew that, deep down. I've seen other conservative Christians make this same pivot time and time again. When the chips are down—when men and women face death squarely in the face—they often discover their own hidden need for a miracle-working God. And it makes sense, too, for where else can a person turn? Who better to defeat the specter of death than the Spirit that raised Christ from the dead?

My elders came over. We surrounded his bed. We took out a small bottle of oil and anointed his head. We prayed loud, bold prayers. We spoke in tongues. And all the while, Dad laid there, eyes closed, praying right along with us.

It didn't take long. Dad felt something and sat up.

"I'm healed," he said. "I feel better! Jesus just touched me!"

My mom shook her head. "Oh honey, he did not. We need to take you to the hospital."

"No, I don't! I'm telling you, I know I'm healed!"

I told Dad to go to the hospital anyway to get checked out. If he really was healed, the cardiologist could confirm it.

And he did.

Dad really had suffered a heart attack, the cardiologist confirmed. But by the looks of it, he had completely recovered. It was inexplicable.

"What in the world happened to you?" the cardiologist said.

"I called for my son to pray, and he did. Jesus healed me!"

The doctor shrugged. I don't know if he believed him or not, but he smiled and said, "Well, good for you then."

When Dad came home, he went to his medicine cabinet and threw away all his medication, and from that day on, he grew stronger. It was a miracle. But it was more than a simple healing. In one day, God mended my Dad's heart in two places. Not only were his arteries healed, but our relationship was suddenly, dramatically restored at the same time. God gave me back my father that day.

As evidence to that fact, Dad went to the next elders meeting at Harrisburg Christian. Those meetings had largely evolved, I was told, into closed-door Jon Bowers bashing sessions. A lot of people had left the church, you see, in favor of Christ's Center, and the elders were blaming me for loss in numbers. My Dad stepped into that meeting and said, "From now on I never want to hear my son's name mentioned negatively. Ever."

And from then on, Dad was an ally. A friend. We remained very close for the rest of his life.

God was not finished in his work of restoration, however. In truth, it had only just begun.

This was an incredible season in our lives. God was giving us back the relationships we had all but given up for dead. One after another they came, each one asking for forgiveness.

Dr. Bill Richardson, the same seminary professor who had determined I was either demon possessed or having a breakdown, was one of the first to call. He had been a friend of mine up until that point, and we hadn't spoken since.

"Jon, I need to repent to you. I did something awful." This was a full year after I had left the church.

I smiled into the phone and said, "Well, I happen to know what it was." Then, he asked for my forgiveness, and I was more than happy to give it to him.

"Jon, the truth is, I didn't know what to think," he explained. "I had just never seen God move like he was moving through you, so

I agreed with the elders and made an assumption. I was wrong, and I'm glad for what God is doing in your life."

My old friend Bill Morris came around, too. Bill had been a steadfast elder at Harrisburg Christian, and he owned a thriving local business in the area, but our relationship had ended when I left. But one day, Bill sent me a heartfelt letter of apology.

"I realize what we did as an eldership was wrong," he wrote, and he enclosed a substantial check for Christ's Center Church.

The two of us spoke many times after that about the power of the Holy Spirit. Bill always regretted what the church had done. He saw it as more than a simple relational breakdown. In His mind, God had sent a gift to Harrisburg Christian church—the gift of the Holy Spirit. But in casting me aside, they had cast that gift aside as well.

Bill was a wonderful man. Even in the thick of the controversy, he had been the one to stick up for me. In that fateful elder's meeting, he alone had proposed that I might, in fact, be right. To forgive a man like that was a great delight.

But of all the restorative works God did in that season, the most dramatic was with Merril Rush. Merril was the one who had delivered the elder's original decree that I was demon possessed or having a breakdown. I had always loved this man and his wife, Beulah. Losing that relationship had hurt worse than most.

One day, Sunday afternoon, Beulah called me. Merril wanted to see me, she said. He had suffered a stroke.

I went to see them, and Beulah met me at the door and gave me her traditional hug. She had known me since I was a little boy. She had been my Sunday school teacher and had hugged me more times than I could count over the years. For her to embrace me at that moment was a comfort to me.

She lowered her voice. "Jon, Merril believes he's going to meet the Lord soon, and God spoke to him today and...well, I'll let him tell you what God said." She led me into the room where he sat, and I'll be honest, he didn't look good. His right eye was closed, he was drooling down the right side of his face, and there were sores on his head. Shingles.

"Jonny, sit down beside me," he said. I did. "Jonny, I'm going to go home. I'm going to see God. So, I asked Him this morning if there was anybody I've offended and needed to repent to. He told me there was. He said, "'Jon Bowers. He said He sent you to Harrisburg Christian as a gift, but we did not receive you."

"Jonny, I know God is right. We did not receive you. Will you please forgive me?"

I smiled. "Yes. I forgive you, Merril."

"Good," he said. "Good. Now I'm going to ask you for something else. I never thought I'd say this, but I'm going to." He swallowed. "Jonny, can you give me what you've got?"

My jaw fell open. I knew what he meant. "Merril, do you know what you're asking?"

"Probably not. But I want the power that I've watched God work in your life. I'm going home, Jonny, and I don't want to go home weak. I want to go home strong!"

It was a brave request from a brave man. "Okay, Merril," I said. "Then I'm going to ask God to give you the gifts of the Holy Spirit including the gifts of tongues and discernment. I'm going to ask Him to give you all the gifts. Is that okay with you?"

He nodded. He was ready. A brave man indeed.

Normally, in such circumstances, I lay hands on a person. That's the way Jesus did it, that's the way they did it in the New Testament, and that's good enough for me. But this time was different. I didn't want to lay hands on my old friend, courageous soul through he be. That's because of his shingles. His entire head was an open sore. His hair looked like it was matted with honey.

God saw my revulsion and spoke forcefully to my heart. "You lay hands on his head!"

Fine, I told him. And I reached out and touched his head. My hand was stuck there for an instant.

Then, I started praying in tongues, asking God to fill my old friend with His Holy Spirit, to fill him with all his gifts, including the gift of healing. Yes, I know Merril was ready to meet God face to face, but I wasn't ready to give him up yet. Not when God had just restored our friendship.

As I was praying, something utterly unexpected happened. Beulah started dancing. She was jumping up and down, shouting out a melody I had never heard. She was twirling, and shouting. She was suddenly full of the Holy Spirit.

It was a collateral blessing. I had prayed for Merril to be filled, and God had filled his wife. Merril though didn't feel anything.

I went home and didn't hear anything from him until a month later when my mom called me. "Did you hear about Merril? The doctors said he never had a stroke!" So of course, I had to go over and investigate.

Beulah met me at the front door and swooped me up into her familiar, reassuring hug. Only this time, there was no hint of sadness in it. It was pure joy.

Merrill was in the living room. He stood up when I entered the room. His shingles were gone, and his smile was full on both sides. His heavy head of white hair was perfectly combed and shampooed. And his formerly paralyzed hand was waving in the air.

He wore a massive grin. "Jonny, tell me! Tell me Jesus doesn't heal today!"

We laughed and praised God together. This was not the same shell of a man I had prayed for. Here was a healthy man with full command of both hemispheres of his body. It was utterly impossible.

Impossible, like what God had done with my father.

Impossible, like buying the church building with a low bid.

Impossible, like the mending of marred hearts and ruined relationships.

Indeed, the Holy Spirit is the God of the impossible. And this particular healing left an indelible mark on my spirit. Maybe it was the dramatic external turnaround I saw which no one could deny. Maybe it was the feeling of the sticky wound on my hand. Maybe it was the sense that this was a holistic restoration. Whatever it was, the healing and infilling of Merril Rush became a foundational moment in my early ministry. For years after that, any time I felt anxious or overwhelmed, any time I felt the sting of doubt creeping in, I would hear the Lord whisper, "Drive over to Merril's house." I would. And I would sit out there and reflect on that moment.

"Just look at what God has done," I would tell my spirit. And in that reminder, I would find my faith restored. God would give me back the broad boldness of an overcomer.

Not only was Merril filled with healing and the Holy Spirit, but he also became a strong supporter of me and my ministry after that, just as Jim, my Dad, Dr. Richardson, and Bill Morris had. There were others, too. So many others. God had restored to us all that was taken away through the enemy's seeds of discord.

I want to be clear about this, too, God did a great healing work in Harrisburg Christian Church as well. That congregation still exists today, and they are doing wonderful things for the Lord. Their current pastor, a man of God named Clare, called my office one day sometime in the mid-1990s. He and Bill Morris wanted to meet for lunch. It had been twenty years since the church had excused me.

"Jon, I have heard the stories," Clare said, "but I want to hear it from you. Did our church really throw you out for being filled with the Holy Spirit?"

I pointed to Bill Morris. "Ask Bill. He was there," I said. Bill just shrugged.

"He told me already," Clare said, "but I want to hear it from you."

I nodded. "Yes, pastor, it's true."

Clare was aghast. "I can't believe that happened." Then, he looked at me with earnestness and humility.

"Jon, on behalf of my church, would you please forgive us? That was wrong, and it's not who we are."

It was a beautiful moment of completion. Even though I didn't feel like I necessarily needed more emotional closure, it was powerful to see the healing work of the Holy Spirit. Sometimes He moves quickly, as He had with my father's heart and Merril's nervous system. And sometimes, He plays the long game. Either way, no matter how long the wait, the plans of the enemy cannot stand against Him. The Spirit of God will triumph in due time. He will bring the breakthrough. He will bring the vindication. He will work wonders we never thought we'd see. And each time He does, we have the opportunity to dance like Beulah danced, and to shout aloud like Merril, "Tell me Jesus doesn't heal today!"

Chapter 5: The Castoffs

Trusting God is not like riding a bike. It doesn't stick with you forever after you learned one time. We have to learn it, then relearn it, and each time, it is uncomfortable. If we want to have the kind of faith to make disciples of all nations, we need to become accustomed to feeling uncomfortable. God will challenge us and stretch us. Each time we succeed in trusting Him it doesn't mean we've arrived. It only means we are ready for another challenge.

I had trusted the Holy Spirit in my old church, and I had trusted Him in launching Christ's Center, and He had rewarded that faith. He had vindicated me, and had restored all I had lost. But now there arose a new challenge—to allow God to build this congregation in the way He saw fit.

We were an energetic, healthy bunch in the early 80's. The school was thriving and our people were growing in the Lord. But one day, God spoke something to me in a prayer time that I couldn't shake. He said, "I will give you gifts in strange packages. Ignore the package, and receive the gift."

I knew at once He was talking about people, but I didn't know how to make that happen. You can't just put out a sign on the church marquee that says, "welcome those with strange wrapping paper." And even if you did, it wouldn't make churchgoers feel any better. Church people typically don't like strange packages. They want predictable people who already know how to behave. Strange packages make us uncomfortable. They embarrass us.

Of course, Jesus didn't seem to have such reservations. He accepted all sorts of strange packages. He looked past the reputations and saw the value inside them. There was Mary Magdalene, a woman with a sketchy past, and Matthew, one of those tax collectors everyone assumed was a thief. Then there was Judas, the man who really was a thief, Simon, the former violent Zealot, and Peter the uncouth, loud mouth disciple from the backwater region of Galilee. Jesus did not seem to care about any of their reputations. He simply brought them close. He welcomed them in the same way as He welcomed lepers, soldiers, and Samaritan adulteresses.

If we were to love like Jesus loved, we would have to embrace people just like this—the overlooked, dismissed, and those who have been cast out—people with special needs, checkered histories, and ongoing struggles. And on the one hand, that's easy. Every church should be opening their doors to the misfits and the castoffs, and we never turned anyone away. But God was calling us to go farther than that baseline. He wanted us to welcome them with arms flung open, and to give them a seat at the table.

It was a challenge and a stretch. I wanted to grow the church, and this was not a very good way to do it. Then again, Jesus said in Matthew 16:18, "I will build my church." So maybe it wasn't my job at all. Maybe my only job was to be obedient to what God said. Maybe all I had to do was trust God's instructions and love His people.

"Okay, Lord," I said. "I'll do it. I'll welcome in the gifts in strange packages. So how do I do it?"

When I asked the question, I knew the answer at once. Ed Glaspey. He was the key.

Ed was a dear friend of mine. He and his wife Mona had come with us when we left Harrisburg Christian, had endured the mice running through the rafters of the barn, and had stuck with me through the scary process of launching the new church. Now he was one of my elders.

More importantly, though, Ed had experienced a dramatic overhaul in his life. The Lord had taken him on a wild journey. Ed's marriage had been on the brink. He had been involved in adulterous relationships, and had experienced a severe pornography addiction. Now, he was free from all that, his marriage was restored, and he was happily growing in Christ. He had come out of his brokenness with a deep conviction to help others overcome their own. In fact, he had approached me about starting up a ministry to do just that.

Ed's idea was simple enough. He just wanted to teach a weekly class based on what God had shown him in his own journey toward wholeness. But this was going to be more than that, and I knew it. If we started working with hurting people—I mean really reaching out to them and inviting them into our growing family—people would come, and they would make messes. It was inevitable. That's just what hurting people do. It would be our job, then, to champion them. We would become a church of misfits.

"Ed, I want you to do this," I told him, and Restoration Ministries was born.

Some of the students looked perfectly normal on the outside, but many did not. Drug addicts came. Ex-convicts came. And rigid, Pharisaical Christians came. It wasn't long until we realized many of these students needed more attention than the one night a week class. We needed to expand.

Fortunately, we had space. Our cafeteria building was just big enough to become a makeshift dorm. Before we knew it, Restoration became a live-in discipleship course.

We began teaching classes throughout the week, handing out daily work duties, and providing opportunities for outreach. I wasn't very involved with the classroom part myself—I left that to Ed—but the fallout reached me on a regular basis. There was regular conflict of all kinds, chemical, emotional, and spiritual. There were bitter arguments, fights, angry neighbors, and visits from the local police department. Broken people make messes, like I said.

But there were also beautiful victories taking place. Hurting people were finding freedom, and rejected souls were finding home.

Soon, we discovered "gifts in strange packages" didn't just refer to people who had made a mess of their lives. It also meant people who society had written off unjustly. I'm talking about those with physical and intellectual disabilities. They needed a community of love and acceptance more than they needed a class, but the classes were a bonus. Everyone has past hurts they are dealing with, but people with handicaps are on the receiving end of years of rejection and pain. Churches often grapple with how to accept and accommodate these individuals, but we were ready.

So, the Lord brought us Arden. Arden was a short, little man, that was the first thing you'd notice. He was maybe five feet tall with a rounded girth and scraggly brown hair. The second thing you'd notice was his constantly shifting posture. He would rock back and forth incessantly, with both hands scrunched up at his chest. His fingers were always fluttering. Then you would see his eyes closed, or else pointed upward, shifting this way and that, but landing nowhere. Arden was blind.

Before he came to us, he had spent some time at a blind school in a nearby city, then at a large church in town where he had hoped to settle down and serve as a music minister. He was a pianist, he told us but the church wouldn't allow him to play. Someone suggested he come see us out at Christ's Center, because we had the Restoration school, and we would take him in.

They were right. We did take him. And because we did, we got to enjoy the outrageous gift God had given him.

Picture this—a city inspector comes to investigate our cafeteria-turned-dorm. There had been complaints, and they were threatening to shut us down. So we're walking the inspector through the building, and we run into Arden. We introduce them.

"Arden's our praise leader," we say.

Arden Haidean

The inspector looks him up and down, his face full of doubt. There was no way this funny little man could lead a church congregation in Sunday morning worship.

I smiled. "Play something for him, Arden."

Whenever Arden sat at a piano, his fingers loosened and his hands caught fire. Up and down the scales they would run with effortless flare. He could play like no one I've ever heard. Or maybe it would be more accurate to say he could play like anyone I've ever heard. It didn't matter the composer—Mozart, Beethoven, or Keith Green—he could replicate the music perfectly without breaking a sweat. And it wasn't just the music, either. He could mimic any vocalist you could throw at him. If you closed your eyes, you'd swear you were listening to Elton John.

Arden's unusual appearance had the perfect disarming effect. Nobody ever saw it coming.

That afternoon, I don't remember what Arden played for the inspector, but he thoroughly moved the man. Rattled him, even. Arden's gift, and the place we had made for him, seemed to settle the man's concerns. We passed the inspection, and he left us alone after that.

And just like we told him, Arden led our congregation in worship on Sunday mornings. We all loved it when he would play. He was one of the most talented men I've ever known.

It's difficult to think about Arden without also thinking of his wingman, Michael O'Barr. Michael didn't have prodigious talent like Arden did, but he was, himself, one of the greatest gifts God ever gave to Christ's Center.

One day, a missionary friend from Texas called us and said, "We've got someone that needs help, and we can't help him."

That was a strange thing to say. After all, our friend was a Ywammer—a staff member with Youth With a Mission, the world's largest missions agency. Ywam is known for being able to make disciples of pretty much anybody.

Michael O'Barr

"Who is he?"

"His name is Michael, and he has Down's syndrome."

Michael had gone to YWAM to try to become a missionary. He had a genuine, sweet affection for Jesus that was impossible not to notice. But he also had other traits that were impossible not to notice—namely, he couldn't control his bodily functions at times.

That issue had come to the forefront on his recent outreach to Mexico, causing great embarrassment to Michael and to the church he was visiting.

But Michael's needs went far beyond such physical issues. He had spent much of his life in a state institution where people dictated every moment of his day. Now, he was a thirty-year old adult who lacked confidence and know-how on everything that didn't have to do with Alabama Crimson Tide football.

Once again, it was our Restoration dorm that made us good candidates to take him in, so we said yes. When he arrived, Michael was wearing his red Alabama football sweatshirt. He was short and dark haired with a wide, friendly smile, and his face bore all the expected marks of his genetic condition. When I saw him, the Lord spoke to me, "Love this man. Make him a part of your family." It was not a request, and it was not a general directive for the church. Rather, it was personal.

"Michael from Roebuck." That's what they called him at the local radio station where he grew up in Alabama. He was a regular caller on the local sports programs, and he had a reputation for correcting the hosts on various football statistics, and he was never wrong. His encyclopedic memory made the hosts nervous, and made listeners remember him.

To this day, it's one of the things we remember most about him, too. In fact, it was his love of sports that ultimately gave us the key to helping Michael grow.

Christ's Center School had an active athletic program, and when Michael showed up, we put him right at the center of it. He helped coach the flag football team, and soon, I made him the assistant athletic director.

You might think these were figurehead positions, but Michael had real authority. I made sure of it. Once, when he attended a meeting of athletic directors from our public school district, he caused a bit of a minor stir by granting permission to a smaller school to join our league. The other men hemmed and hawed about that, but he had made the decision in my name. I backed him up, and we moved forward with his commitment.

Working with Michael wasn't always easy. He had an incredible aptitude for some things, including reading and remembering the scriptures, but he had considerable difficulty with menial tasks like sweeping the floor or moving tables. Some of that was due to his disability, but more of it, I think, was because of his history. Back in the institution, they hadn't believed in him. They had merely taken care of him. As a result, he lacked the know-how and the confidence to do things on his own.

"Michael, you're not retarded," we told him. "You're unique!" We did our best to help him see his uniqueness, and to walk in the confidence of one who knew he was loved by his heavenly Father. Over time, such encouragements started to make a real difference.

When Michael met Arden, the two of them became friends, and made up one of the most hilarious and unlikely duos you'd ever see. They both lived in the Restoration dorm, and were fixtures around the church and school. I often took them with me when I went to meetings or weddings or even on outreaches, but even when I didn't, they were still together often. Michael was Arden's set of eyes, and Arden was Michael's wallet.

They drove each other crazy, of course. Once, we picked them up a couple of blocks from the church. Arden was so upset he was swinging his cane in Michael's direction. We asked them what the problem was.

"He was walking too fast," Arden complained.

But Michael countered, "I was hungry, and he was walking too slow!"

As Michael began to mature into a higher functioning adult, he also began to speak more boldly about his love for Jesus.

"Jon, I want to preach," he said to me one day, and I let him do it. It was the shortest sermon in Christ's Center history, but it didn't matter. When Michael got up in front of an audience, something happened deep inside all of our hearts. Just as Arden had the ability to move an audience with his musical genius, so Michael could melt them with his unwavering joy.

"I sure do love and appreciate you all," he would begin when he got on stage. And he meant it, too. He did love them. He loved everybody.

Then, he would say something like this: "I'm not a speaker, but let me tell you, I'm happy. A lot of you guys have a lot of blessings. You've got a car, and you've got a wife, but you're still not happy. I don't have a car because I can't afford one, and I can't drive anyway. And I probably won't ever get married. But you know what? I'm still happy."

How was he so happy? It was because of Jesus, he would say. The joy of the Lord. It was that simple.

The audience could see at once that this young man was richer than they were. He walked in a contentedness most people don't understand. So their hearts would sink, and tears would fill their eyes.

It happened every time.

Then he would ask them, "Are you as happy as I am? Because if you're not, I'll pray for you." So they would come forward, and he would pray for them. And when they left the building, they would remember what happened. They would remember his joy.

Christ's Center became a stronger place because of the Michaels and the Ardens. These men had no pretension about them. They simply loved Jesus and wanted community.

The same could be said for the others in the Restoration class: the reforming legalists, the recovering alcoholics, the depressed and the angry. They loved God, and they wanted people to stand next to them and say, "I believe in you." Indeed, the only difference between these folks and "regular" religious people is that these ones actually knew they were broken, and they were willing to let God put them back together.

So while Ed taught them how to find breakthrough, our church leadership kept them close. We invited them into our homes and spent long, extended hours together. We traded encouragement over the lunch table. We challenged them, and then put them in places where they could succeed.

Still, not everybody was happy about it. I started to hear the grumblings early on. Our neighbors wanted us to close the Restoration school, and they weren't alone. People in the church—our more straight-laced, peace keeping members—wanted us to kick them out. They had valid concerns, but most of them, I dare say, were rooted in fear, and I was not about to give into fear.

Finally, some of our own church leaders confronted me in my office. They had had enough, and they gave me an ultimatum: "Either Ed Glaspey and Restoration goes, or we go."

I wasn't surprised, but I was angry. They knew better.

So, I took a deep breath and told them to leave the building. As for me and my house, we already made our choice, we would fear the Lord. We would follow His lead even if He led us into messy places. Trusting God would be a risky venture, but heaven's reward was always bigger than the investment.

Ever since those early days when we hosted the Restoration dorm, Christ's Center has been a home for the broken. I think we have Michael to thank for that. When I put him in a place to succeed, he blossomed in a way that left an indelible mark on our congregation. Even to this day, the church welcomes the hurting, the depressed, and those with special needs. It's a part of the congregation's DNA.

And as it turns out, this is how God built his church. He knew what He was doing, and in some ways, I think the joke was on us. We were *all* gifts in strange packages after all, and God knit our hearts together in powerful ways. Thus, Christ's Center became a community of the broken people in the midst of God's redemption. And because we embraced that calling, He blessed us in ways I would never have expected.

Chapter 6: Winning Souls

Back when I used to sneak into services at Eugene Faith Center to get a taste of the Holy Spirit, Roy Hicks, Jr. would ask this question: "How many people have you led to the Lord this week?"

Before then, I had never thought much about sharing my faith. I hardly ever told people about Jesus, and I didn't consider it a central part of being a Christian. But Roy's challenge alerted me to the urgency and centrality of sharing the gospel. Suddenly, I wanted to lead people to Jesus. In fact, I felt I had wasted years of my life as a believer by not actively sharing my faith. I was tired of attending funerals with a vague sense of guilt. I was ready to make up for lost time.

Early in my tenure as pastor of Christ's Center, I decided to make a concerted effort to lead people around the community to Jesus. And the more I did that, the more other things happened, strange, exciting "God-things." Soul winning became a magnet for the supernatural.

Here's one example. One afternoon, I got a call from the superintendent of the Harrisburg School District, a man named Red Crabb. I had known Red since I was a boy. He had moved from Oklahoma in the second grade, and had gone on to lead Harrisburg High School to the high school basketball state championship. I was in grade school then, and he had been one of the athletes I had looked up to. Now, as superintendent of the district, the entire town looked up to him.

Red wasn't a Christian, but everybody loved him. He had a trademark; easy-going way about him, for every situation he had a wise and homespun saying from his native Oklahoma. But more than that, people loved Red because they knew he cared for them. He later said, "If I hadn't met Jesus, I would have been the nicest man in hell." It's probably true.

On the afternoon Red called me, he wanted to come to my office to sell me on Amway—an immensely popular multi-level marketing company back then. I told him to come on over, sensing there was something more to this meeting. God was in it somehow. I could feel it.

When he stepped into my office we shook hands. He was smiling that big, infectious smile he is so famous for.

We stepped into my office, but right as he began his sales pitch, I cut him off. "Red Crabb," I said, "You did not come here to sell me Amway."

He stopped. "I didn't?"

"No, Red. You came here to get saved."

It was a risk. A relational risk. But evangelism requires boldness.

Red looked puzzled. "Saved... from what?"

I told him the whole thing as simply as I could. I told how we're all sinners and deserved punishment, but Jesus died to take the punishment on his own shoulders. If we put our trust in His salvation, we could inherit the new life of the resurrection.

He thought about it. I could see in his eyes that he needed it. Wanted it. The Holy Spirit was stirring deep in his heart, but Red didn't move.

"Jon, would you just pray for me?" He said.

"No," I responded. "I wouldn't pray for you for anything. If you want it, you get down on your knees and ask for it yourself."

The words just flew out of my mouth. They sounded harsh, but I knew they were right. Red needed this challenge. He couldn't receive a restored relationship with God by proxy. He had to invite God into his life himself.

The next moment he was on the floor, his eyes squeezed shut. He told me later he felt scared, as if a deep darkness was swirling all around him, pulling him in. And indeed, there probably was. The moment of decision is a moment of warfare. The angels are on the edge of celebration, and the demons, on the verge of a loss, tend to dig their talons in deeper.

I sensed he needed help, so I put my hand on his shoulder. "It's easy, Red. Just repeat after me."

I led him in a simple prayer of repentance and invitation, often called "the sinner's prayer." There is nothing magic about any prayer, but if any prayer is prayed with an honest heart, God hears it and responds.

God responded that day. He overwhelmed Red with the glory of new life in Jesus. Soon, my friend was weeping with gladness. His soul was won.

Red's decision to follow Jesus set off a chain reaction in his family. It started the same day, when Red came home to his wife, Loveta. He told her what had happened. "I just gave my life to Jesus Christ," he said, still a little amazed by it all.

"I sure hope that happens to me some day," she said.

And his brother Kenny told him the same thing that evening at a local football game. "I've got to have that," he said.

This got Red thinking. If his own wife wanted to meet Jesus, and his brother wanted to meet Jesus, and his brother's wife Shirley wanted to meet Jesus (he hadn't actually talked with her, but he thought she probably felt the same way). Well then, he should make sure they could meet Jesus. But he didn't quite know what to do, so he called me over.

I met all four of them together, and I led them in the same, simple prayer I had led Red in. Joy, tears, and gladness ensued. Three new souls surrendered and set free. God was transforming an entire family.

But there was another brother. A younger brother named Tom. He was the rowdy one with somewhat of a reputation for being a rabble-rouser.

But I wasn't intimidated by any of that. I told him he needed to get right with God. I invited him to accept Jesus.

"Jon, you don't understand," he said. "I like to drink beer and raise hell."

I smiled and shrugged. "Well, don't let *that* keep you out of heaven."

He walked away that day with all the appearance of hardness. He hadn't necessarily listened, but he still heard me.

Red had made similar overtures toward his brother, but Tom had responded with the kind of hostility and profanity often reserved for brothers. He didn't want any part of it.

"That's okay," Red said. "But I can't imagine being in heaven without you."

I think our interactions with Tom must have rolled around in his head the following weeks. Finally, one night, when he was fully loaded with alcohol—or "drunk as a skunk," as Red described him—Tom heard someone mention the name of Jesus in the middle of the bar, and he knew what he needed to do. He staggered off his stool and somehow, by the grace of God, made it over to his brother Red's house.

It was late, but Red wasn't surprised to see him at that hour, or in that pitiful state. "What do you need?" Red asked him.

"You know what I need," Tom said. He was loaded down with guilt. "I need you to pray for me."

Red would have deferred to me in that situation, but I was at home, of course. So, being a brand new believer himself, Red reached for the only words that were familiar to him for this kind of situation. He told his brother, "I wouldn't pray for you for anything. If you want it, you get down on your knees and ask for it yourself."

Tom obeyed. He got on his knees and prayed an earnest prayer of repentance and submission to Jesus. What happened next was strange and wonderful—Tom not only received Jesus, he got up off the floor a sober man, lucid and completely in his right mind.

Red would say later that the first miracle he ever saw happened that night, when Jesus turned wine back into water. Tom was never pulled back toward alcoholism. The moment he turned his life over to God, he was set free. He is a pastor to this day, and he specializes in leading rabble-rousers like himself to Jesus.

That story demonstrates a phenomenon I have observed over and over again regarding miracles and salvations—in my experience, they often go together. God's wonders frequently accompany the sharing of the gospel.

Of course, I didn't come up with this idea. The New Testament reports it rather plainly at the close of Mark's Gospel… "And they went out and preached everywhere, while the Lord worked with them, and confirmed the word by the signs that followed." Mark 16:20 Signs and wonders were meant to be a confirmation of the message of the gospel. It is no coincidence that the day the Holy Spirit came down with tongues of supernatural fire was the same day three thousand souls were saved. Nor should we be surprised when Philip baptized the Ethiopian eunuch, he was at once transported to another town entirely. Miracles and salvation make a great pairing.

Maybe this is one of the reasons we don't see many healings today in the west. Maybe it has nothing to do with dispensations or apostolic ages and more to do with our own weak evangelistic tendencies. Maybe if we regained our sense of boldness to share the gospel in modern America, then God would confirm that boldness with prophetic outpourings, words of knowledge, tongues, healing, and deliverance.

God was confirming His word to us back then, and He was doing it often. It only made me more excited to share the good news of the risen Savior. I felt God had impressed me with a specific goal to lead at least one person to Christ every week, in agreement with Roy Hicks' earlier challenge. It was a tall order, but I didn't have to do it alone. God brought me a tremendous ally.

When Red Crabb gave his life to Christ, something wonderful began. He started attending Christ's Center, and he told me he immediately felt as if he had found his home. I was thrilled, and the two of us became closer friends.

Soon, I worked up the nerve to make Red a ridiculous offer. I asked him to come join our staff. I asked him to leave his lucrative position as the Harrisburg superintendent to come run our small Christian school. It made no sense, of course. I could only offer him a fraction of the salary he earned through the district, and there were no benefits.

Still, he said yes. Why did he do it? It was sheer faith. He didn't know what the future held, but he believed God was walking with him and would take care of him.

The fact that Red could display such faith so early in his Christian walk was of great encouragement to me. I wanted to surround myself with people who were willing to follow God, even when the odds were against them. Red Crabb fit that bill. He was a risk taker. So when I asked Red to join me on an unusual weekly quest to find and save lost souls, he didn't hesitate.

Every Monday, we went on a weekly treasure hunt of sorts along in my old pick up truck, a classic, green three-quarter ton '76 Chevy Silverado. We had bought the truck for the farm a few years earlier, and it quickly became my favorite vehicle. Someone had given it the nickname, "Old Greeny,"even though it was new, and the name stuck.

Every Monday, Old Greeny took Red and me up and down the streets of Harrisburg, and we would ask the Lord, "Who do you want us to preach the Gospel to today?" And He would tell us, and we would go. It was that simple.

But it was also a risk. Between the two of us, Red and I knew more or less every person in town. Whether that made things easier or harder is difficult to say. When people know all about your pedigree and history, and you know theirs, inquiries about the state of their souls can get awkward pretty quickly. Maybe that was why Jesus sent out his disciples two by two in the first place. When there are two of you, it's easier to push through any potential awkwardness and help "keep your eyes on the prize," as the song says. And, time and again, God gave us prizes.

"Go see the Lynch family," He said on one of those Mondays. Again, this was not some kind of audible voice, but I heard Him in my spirit. The Lynch family had been in the area for many years. Plez and Nina were elderly farmers, and well-regarded members of the community. But they did not know Jesus.

We showed up on their doorstep, and told them why we were there. We wanted to introduce them to Jesus. Sometimes, such conversations can stretch on for hours. Not this time. This time, we found their hearts were ready and open. Apparently, God had already been drawing them to Himself, and preparing them for this moment of decision. Such Divine coordination should come as no surprise. It is Christ who always makes the first move, drawing us in subtle, sometimes imperceptible ways. God plants seeds in lost souls, gently nudging them toward Himself with all kinds of tools like casual conversations, a lingering question, or a simple act of kindness by a believing friend. It takes years sometimes, but when those seeds sprout and start to blossom, God often brings in a pair of harvesters in a green pick up truck.

Plez and Nina wept as they received Jesus. And when they were done weeping, Plez looked up and said, "Will you two do me a favor? Will you drive over to my son's house and lead him to the Lord?"

We said yes, of course. We were happy to. So happy, in fact, that we jumped into Greeny and got a good ways down the road before we realized neither one of us knew where their son, George, lived.

There were no mobile phones in this day, of course, so we couldn't just call Plez and Nina. We could have turned around and driven back, but just then, I got thirsty. Out of nowhere, my stomach clenched, and I couldn't keep on going.

"Red, I have got to get something to drink before we keep going."

So we stopped at the familiar truck stop and restaurant by the freeway. We got out of Greeny, and when we walked through the door, we saw him. George Lynch. He was sitting in a booth next to his wife, Maudie, having dinner. The moment I saw them, my thirst up and vanished. I didn't need a drink anymore. Had God given me that thirst just to lure us to that spot?

George smiled and waved us over.

"Jon and Red, good to see you guys!"

"Good to see you," I said. "Do you know where we just were?" And I proceeded to tell them both all about our visit to their parent's house. I told them how they had just received Jesus, and wanted the same for George.

Their expressions were markedly different. Maudie glowed with joy.

"That's wonderful!" she exclaimed.

But George just shifted in his chair and folded his arms. "Well, I think I'm all right."

It is a good wife who knows the heart of her husband. Maudie knew George, and she wasn't about to let him get off so easily.

"No, George, you are not all right!" she protested.

And she was correct. George needed Jesus. It didn't take long for his defenses to crumble. Then, he was ready. Maudie was ready, too. They both bowed their heads and surrendered their lives to Jesus right there in that booth at the truck stop. All because I got unbearably thirsty at precisely the right moment.

God used my unusual physical thirst to bring about a salvation, and an entire family came to Him in a single afternoon.

George passed away six months later. I didn't know it then, but this would become a pattern. Many of those people we led to Jesus on those Monday afternoons died soon after. I was honored to conduct many of their funeral services. God was being gracious to these souls, drawing them to Himself at the eleventh hour. I am thankful that I listened for His voice.

Around that time I started keeping a log of everyone I shared the gospel with. I wrote down their names and the date, and I made a note if and when they became believers. Sometimes I was met with hardness and harsh words. Other times, people listened politely but don't respond at all.

But rather than getting put off or disappointed by the rebuttals, I pressed on for the sake of people like Red, Tom, and George, people whose hearts were already being drawn by the Holy Spirit. And because He is the very same Spirit that raised Christ from the dead, strange and amazing things often happened surrounding those conversations.

Because evangelism became a cornerstone of our ministry at Christ's Center Church, I don't think it's any coincidence that we saw God accomplish so many impossible things. Today, looking back on it all, I am more convinced than ever of this correlation—if you want to see a miracle, go share the gospel.

Chapter 7: The Outpouring

I was driving a heavy, rickety bus down a long and sprawling hill in Tijuana Mexico, trying to keep calm. Behind me was a gaggle of Christ's Center high school students on a mission. Some of them were still in face paint after an afternoon of open-air drama ministry. They were having a great time reliving the day's events, smiling and laughing like always. They had no idea we were in danger. I was the only one who knew. I found Red Crabb's face in the overhead mirror and motioned him forward. Red slipped out of his seat and walked down the aisle, crouching down next to me.

"Don't react," I told him. "But we have a problem."

He leaned in. "What's up?"

I swallowed. "We don't have any brakes."

I can still feel it—the sensation of being powerless and completely at the mercy of forces greater than me. It was a scary feeling, but not altogether unfamiliar. Back in Oregon, I had felt the same thing when the Spirit of God was poured out over Christ's Center School.

We had been doing well, both in the church and in the school. On Sunday, the worship was strong, and on Monday through Friday we were doing our very best to prepare children for adulthood. Our teachers were good, because they loved the kids. Even our basketball program was thriving. It was a blessed time.

But there is a human tendency in the midst of blessed seasons to lean in too much on routine expectations. There is a temptation to settle. In some ways, we fell into that. We knew what we had to deliver, and we delivered it, but we stopped there.

I can still remember how vividly it worked in my own life. In the entrance of our school, there was a world map. I would walk by it every day, and I would hear the words from David's second Psalm, "Ask of me, and I will give you nations as your inheritance."

I felt like God was calling me—daring me, even—to lift my gaze, and dream for more. I felt like that call was almost literal, as if He was offering me an opportunity to affect an entire nation.

But the idea of nations was, frankly, overwhelming. I didn't know how to process it. The thought was just too big.

Day after day, I walked past that map and smothered the call.

One evening, though, something unexpected happened. There was a class in the gymnasium for the adults, and I was with the high-school students down in the cafeteria. We were singing, praying, and talking all about the Holy Spirit. Then, out of nowhere, He arrived.

It was all a bit chaotic at first. Some students began weeping. Others began falling over in the middle of prayers. Still others became overwhelmed by the joy of the Lord, and began to laugh or speak in tongues. I had seen the gifts of the Spirit in action before, of course, so I wasn't afraid of the manifestations. But I was also keenly aware that I was not the one driving any of it. These were young people in my charge, and I couldn't control what was going on. I couldn't smother this kind of thing.

As "shepherds" most pastors feel a pressing need to keep their sheep safe. It is a good and holy desire. But left unchecked, that motivation can also stop good things from happening. When faced with situations bigger than them, pastors can get scared that their people will get hurt or confused. They don't want anyone to walk out the door or fall under the spell of some untested leader, so they shut the whole thing down. This is, in fact, exactly what happened to me at my old church in Harrisburg.

My personal reservations aside, I knew I couldn't make the same mistake as a leader. I had to let God's Spirit do whatever He wanted to do.

At the end of the night, I went into the auditorium and told the adults, "there's a move of God's Spirit that you need to be aware of. I want to prepare you. The Holy Spirit fell on your kids tonight. I want you all to go get your kids and bring them in here." They did. And instead of fizzling out, everything intensified. The parents, too, began to speak in tongues, and fall down under the power of God. That meeting went on into the wee hours of the night.

There was no way to have regular school the next day. We just continued to pray and seek God, and He continued to pour His Spirit over us. Even then, I tried to bring some measure of order to the scene, but every time I did, it would start breaking out somewhere else, so I gave up.

On and on it went, and word began to spread. Some parents were angry. They called the whole thing a bunch of "hocus pocus," and told me not to brainwash the kids. I told them I wasn't making any of it happen. If they were upset, they could take it up with God Himself.

One dad came into my office to confront me, and I asked him if I could lay hands on him and pray. He reluctantly agreed. I put my hands on his shoulder and invited the Holy Spirit to come. Immediately, the man fell backwards and hit his head on the door.

Embarrassed, he quickly climbed to his feet and claimed he didn't feel anything. So I laid hands on him again, and again he fell backwards. After that, he got angry, still claiming he couldn't feel a thing and stormed out. He left his child in the school, however. I thought that was a telling decision.

That was the start of a powerful season. God's presence was palpable, and He seemed to bless everything we touched. Some people left the church, of course, but on the whole, our numbers grew, and our services became less predictable. Word got out that God was doing something, so lots of hungry and curious people showed up. In that environment, the unexpected happened. The impossible happened.

One Sunday, in the middle of the worship service, one of our young mothers started screaming, "My baby's dead! My baby's dead!"

Worship stopped at once, and several ladies ran over to aid her. At first, I thought it couldn't be true. But when I saw the baby's face, I knew she was right. My cousin was a coroner, and I had been with him at his work enough to recognize that lifeless expression I can only call a "death mask." That's what I saw on the baby's face.

Someone called for paramedics. I had been trying to lead worship, but now I didn't know what to do.

"Jesus, what now!" I cried in my heart. Then, at once, I knew the answer.

"Friends, we're going to sing a loud praise to God, right now! Together!"

And we did. The whole congregation broke out into a desperate cry of praise to God. Next minute, the baby was interrupting our song with cries of her own.

It was an unforgettable moment.

There were other interruptions, too. One night, we prayed in one of the church classrooms, and we were getting into it. We were praying the words of Acts 2, asking for God's fire to fall on us. Then, all of a sudden, we heard sirens. Lots of them. They were getting closer, and finally, they stopped outside our building.

The firemen got out and walked the halls, inspecting every room for flames. But they found nothing, despite the fact that one of our neighbors across the street had assured them she had seen the building on fire.

"I'm not crazy, Jon." she told me later. "Flames were pouring out of the roof. I know what I saw." Indeed, there had been flames. But those flames were of a different sort, and they were pouring down, not up. The fire of the Spirit was rushing in, not out. The Lord had heard our invitations, and He was responding. But that poor woman was so shaken by her vision, she ended up moving out of state.

The Christian school continued in this direction for some time. Regular extended prayer meetings started forming. Our students began sharing the gifts God had poured out on them around town. They would even ask, "Do you know Jesus?" on the basketball court. That was my idea. Not all of them appreciated that, but they asked anyway.

Speaking of basketball, I would be remiss if I didn't tell the story of the young point guard who played for McKenzie, one of Christ Center's rivals. The kid was good, one of the best in the conference. But during his senior year, he broke his leg, ending his season.

We were playing McKenzie the very next week. The poor kid hobbled into our gymnasium with a cast and crutches. I felt terrible for him.

During the junior varsity game, I went over to his coach and asked him a question.

"Would you mind if our guys took him into the office to pray for him?"

I asked his father, too, and both men agreed. They didn't think it would do any harm, I guess.

So we took him into our pastoral offices, and I had the senior basketball squad anoint his leg with oil, and pray for God's healing, and that was the end of it. Our guys went out and played the varsity game, and we won. Those guys couldn't beat us without their star player.

Several days later, the athletic director called our office and talked to Red Crabb. That young man, it turns out, felt better immediately after we prayed for him, and began asking his dad to go back to the doctor for another x-ray. His dad essentially rolled his eyes at him. They had just taken x-rays. The boy had a broken leg.

Still, the son persisted. He said when the team had prayed for him, his leg felt like it was healed. His dad scoffed. There was no healing. It was pure emotionalism!

Finally, the son prevailed. They took another x-ray, and his leg was strong and unharmed. There was no break. Not anymore. God had healed him through the prayers of his rivals.

And wouldn't you know it? That same boy finished out the year on the basketball team, and he hit the game winning shot against us at the last game of the year. It seems God does have a sense of humor.

I don't mean to give the impression that it was always crazy like that. These things seem to come in waves. Seasons. Just as God had blessed us with a fruitful, exciting season when the Bible study started in my barn, so He had visited us again with an outpouring of fresh wind and fire. It changed us all. And in the midst of it came a settled conviction that we needed to share what God had given us, not only with our community, but with people far away.

Of course, Jesus had commanded His disciples to do that very thing on the day he left them: "Go therefore and make disciples of all the nations, baptizing them in the name of the Father and the Son and the Holy Spirit, teaching them to observe all that I commanded you." (Matt 28:19-20). As a church and a school, we had done some things right, but we hadn't done much about taking the gospel out. We were good at the "making disciples" part, but not at the "going." If we had kept on in that fashion, we would have inevitably become stagnant; never giving out in the same measure as we have received. But I knew we were headed there if we didn't start taking the Great Commission seriously.

And so, we decided to take our students on an outreach. I wasn't ready to ask God for a nation, but that was okay. I didn't see the need to. We already had a location in mind.

Back in the 1980's, short-term church outreaches were not as common as they are today, but most of the parents gave permission to let us take their kids down to San Diego and across the border into Tijuana, Mexico. We made arrangements with some contacts down there, and we knew we could easily do some open-air evangelism, among other things.

On the day before our flight, our contact and host backed out without warning. Suddenly, we had nothing—no place to stay, no transportation, nothing. But we weren't about to cancel, so we kept making phone calls until we found a woman who agreed to pick us up on the Mexican side of the border. She said she had a ride for us, along with duplexes for our team to stay in.

But of course, things never work out the way you plan. When we arrived in San Diego, we got a ride to the border, and we crossed on foot without a problem. Then, we pushed our pile of luggage to the other side of the fence and waited. This woman was supposed to be waiting with a bus, but nobody was there. So we sat on our suitcases and shrugged.

Outreaches are wonderful. I love them. Every time I go, these trips present me with a new opportunity to trust God. When there's no way for you to fix a situation, sometimes you just have to send up a prayer and say, "Lord, I hope you know what you're doing!" This was one of those times.

Finally, at eleven o'clock at night, a bus arrived, if you want to call it a bus. In truth, it was a rickety piece of junk, barely roadworthy. But it was our ride. I'm sure I smiled and said, "Well? Praise God."

We piled in and started down the road. Our driver, though, was beyond terrible. One of the worst I've ever seen. After he ran another car clean off the road, we dismissed him, and I took over. I wasn't about to let him endanger our kids.

It was late when we finally arrived, and we were exhausted. All we wanted was to collapse on a bed—or even a floor—and fall asleep. Unfortunately the duplexes they took us to were not only uncomfortable, they were darn near terrifying. Bugs and cockroaches crawled all over the floor, and everything was utterly filthy.

Somehow, though, we made it to sleep that night, and spent the majority of the next day cleaning up our temporary home. We scrubbed the floors and the walls and chased out the cockroaches as well as we could, and then began our ministry in earnest.

Long before we ever left Oregon, the kids had prepared an evangelistic drama called Zion. They had learned it from a Youth With a Mission team who had used it on outreaches just like this one. There were no words in the drama, but through music and movement, it made clear the story of relationship with God, the entrance of sin, and salvation through Christ. Since hardly any of us spoke Spanish, we figured a drama like this would be a good tool to communicate the gospel.

Performances were easy enough to pull off. All we needed was our small sound system and a little rectangle of land for a makeshift stage. We performed it around the city, in parks, and even in the garbage dump. Every time we did it, these strange gringos in black clothes and white face paint would puzzle people. They would stop and pay attention. And within minutes, they would see themselves in the story. Just like the main character in the drama, they, too, had lost their innocence. They, too, had walked away from God. And they, too, had a shot at redemption.

We would give altar calls after performances, and people always responded. One day, a young man sat and watched the whole thing from a park bench with his girlfriend. We invited people to come meet Jesus, or come get prayer for something else.

"Can Jesus heal my ear?" he asked through an interpreter. He had been suffering from a terrible ear infection. Of course, we had seen enough to know by now that He could, so the students surrounded the couple, laid hands on him, and prayed. And within moments he fell flat on the ground under the power of the Holy Spirit. His girlfriend didn't know what was happening. She started screaming, but it wasn't just because of the fall. Something was coming out of his ears. Green pus, of a sort. It was pouring out of his ear. Some of the ugliest stuff I'd ever seen. It was disgusting. But when he got up off the ground, his ear was totally healed.

It was messy. All of it was messy. But our dignity doesn't seem to be God's chief concern. When the Holy Spirit starts working, I'm not sure He cares much about the clutter, the green ear gunk, or any of our bruised sensibilities. He's too concerned with seeing captives set free. If we try to rush in to control it—to clean it all up too quickly—we're going to miss out. We must trust Him. This is His process. This is His ministry. These are His people. He's the one in control, and we must let Him have the wheel.

And indeed, as Red and I descended that hill in Tijuana with a bus full of young people, we were helpless. The main brakes were completely out, and were about to crash into other vehicles at the intersection below. With no way to safely crash the bus, the only hope we had was the emergency brake and the Holy Spirit. Red grabbed on to both. He pulled with all his might. His face turned the color of his name, and he prayed out in tongues for God to save us.

The bus slowed, jerked, and hissed, then slowed, jerked, and hissed again. It came to a stop just before we crashed into the intersection. And wouldn't you know it? There was a store right there on the corner selling brake fluid.

God was faithful that day. He is still faithful.

Sometimes it's good for us to be powerless. This is one of the great benefits of missions trips. So much can and does go wrong, that we are forced to put ourselves at the mercy of the Holy Spirit. We can fight Him, or we can work with Him, listen for His voice, and hold on with all our might to His coat tails.

That spring in Mexico, we did hold on, and God rewarded our grip with an adventure that none of us would soon forget. That trip whet our appetite for something we hadn't realized we were hungry for. We wanted to go on missions with our God. We wanted to see Him move. And we wanted to move with Him.

Chapter 8: The Heart Attack

All the memories rushed at me in my hospital bed; of Lynna Gay, of our kids, Kim, Todd, and Ryan. Of the old days in Harrisburg, the surprises of the Holy Spirit. Of the outreach to Tijuana, and the similar ones we took shortly after that one.

God had been with us. I had followed His call. From the outside, I had invested my energies well. How could I have only used three talents? It made no sense.

But as God once told the prophet Samuel, "Man looks at the outside appearance, but the Lord looks at the heart." It was there, on the inside, that God saw my weaknesses. He had been trying to get me to pay attention to them, but I hadn't.

Sometimes, it's the subtlest problems that make us crash the hardest. The longer we shove those subtleties aside, the greater they accumulate. That's when they can get dangerous. It is our responsibility, then, to watch our own hearts; to guard them, as the Proverb says; to take stock of how we are responding to what we know is right.

I learned this lesson three painful ways in the early 90's.

The outreach to Tijuana had marked the beginning of a new season for our ministry; one of excitement and exploration. The moment our plane touched down again in Oregon, our kids couldn't stop talking about it. None of us could. We told story after story, both in church and in school, and everyone was energized.

After that, all anyone wanted to talk about was mission trips. We decided we would take the high schoolers on outreaches every spring break, but that wasn't enough. The adults wanted to go too. So, we made opportunities for them to serve as well.

God had been preparing us for our missionary destiny from the beginning. Over the years, we had maintained a close relationship with leaders in various international mission organizations. We had sent out a local boy, Mark Brock, to YWAM (Youth With a Mission) way back in the 70's as Christ's Center's very first missionary, and he had since become a leader at the YWAM training center in East Texas. Through Mark, we met others like my dear friend Wick Nease, brothers who circled the globe with the good news of Jesus Christ. Such men planted seeds of holy adventure in our hearts. Those seeds took years to grow, but now, at last, we were starting to see them bloom. We were waking up to the fact that God had more for us.

Maybe it was that momentum that made us overlook the warning signs. Something was wrong in our community. We were strong in vision, but we were having problems relationally. There was discord among our leadership team, disagreements that were eroding into relational rifts. Those rifts had been there for years, but we had never dealt with them openly. Maybe we thought we could just pray away our difficulties. Maybe we thought that the excitement of the Holy Spirit would be enough to smooth everything over.

Whatever the case, the division didn't heal with time. It only got worse. People say time heals all wounds. To that, my friend Ed Glaspey, in his Restoration teachings, counters, "Time heals nothing." I think he's right. In fact, with relational breakdowns, time sometimes makes things worse.

So it happened that in that season of feverish missionary zeal, the strain on our relationships reached a breaking point, and the church split. There is no need to go into detail as to how it happened. Suffice it to say that good people—men and women of God—disagreed with one another, and found they couldn't go on with the way things were. God was faithful through it all, and as always, He made beauty from it, but that doesn't mean it wasn't hard. It was. Relationships suffered. The church and school suffered, too.

When the dust settled, much had changed. We had more empty seats, and an emptier bank account. Many people were worshipping elsewhere. Plus, our eldership was different, as some of our most prominent figures had left, and I was the only pastor remaining on staff.

But what could we do except keep on going? God didn't give us the option to sit on our hands and wallow in what we lost. He was doing new things, and He was calling us to join Him. So we did. We moved forward with a congregation that was smaller, but a dream that was expanding.

I stayed active during that paradoxical time of pain and acceleration. The balance of family life, ministry, and business was tricky, and I knew it was as important as ever to stay healthy, so I made frequent trips to the gym and the swimming pool. I ran, too, competing regularly in 10K races and half triathlons. As far as middle-aged men were concerned, I was in excellent shape.

Once again, however, outward appearances can be deceiving.

I didn't want to admit it to myself, but the last couple of 10K's I had run had been harder somehow. The breath didn't come as easily as it should have.

That wasn't all, though. I was starting to get aches in my chest. Lynna Gay would bring me Advil, and I would drink them down and shove the matter out of my mind. It was nothing. Just one of those nagging little pains a person hopes will get better with time.

But time heals nothing.

The heart attack came on the day before Easter of 1992. Dry, spring afternoons in Oregon are usually happy affairs. We have to endure long, rainy winters in the Northwest, so when the sunshine finally comes, we soak it in. I was no exception. That afternoon, I was out mowing the lawn. It should have been a perfect day, but instead of glorying in the weather, I was soon out of breath. I felt so winded, I had to stop and try to collect myself on the steps of my house.

Lynna Gay came out and asked what was wrong. Over and over, I tried to fill my lungs with air, but they wouldn't cooperate. And that's when I had to face the thing I had been ignoring. Something was wrong. Something was very wrong. I felt so helpless I started to cry.

"I need to go to the hospital," I admitted at last.

I told the doctors it wasn't a heart attack, but the X-ray proved me wrong. The scans revealed a bleak picture: I had five blockages in my arteries. I would need emergency bypass surgery.

Hours later, I was stretched out on a table, surrounded by the beeping sounds of hospital equipment. And that was when the doctor asked me that fateful question:

"Mr. Bowers, do you have your house in order?"

I was forty-nine years old. I had lived a short life, but my house was was full. Full of gladness. Full of laughter. Full of promise. My wife was my dearest friend, and our children were, and are, our greatest joys.

Pastors often have difficulty balancing family life and ministry. There is a lot of pressure that comes when you take to the pulpit. Some people expect you to have no boundaries. They want you to be available to them twenty-four hours a day, seven days a week, no questions asked. And even though those demanding people are in the minority, pastors often live under the false assumption that everybody feels that way. We end up grappling with things like when to take work home, and when to put it away or when to go to the dance recital, and when to teach that small group? We have to navigate the give-and-take.

For my part, I decided something very early on. My family would always come before my church responsibilities. Always. I decided Lynna Gay was the most important person in the church, and my kids came next. If they weren't happy—if they ever started to feel like they were accessories in my calling as a pastor—I was failing in life. Period.

Thus, I had a policy with them: they could interrupt me in any meeting at any time. They could walk right into my office no matter who was sitting there. I kept a jar of candy on my desk, too, to make sure they would come, and they did. They attended Christ's Center School as they grew, and they would often slip in between classes with a friend and grab a Starburst or a handful of M&M's. It didn't matter if I was meeting with the eldership, or a couple with a broken marriage, or Billy Graham himself. My kids were my priority. They would come first.

That meant I had to be there for them on their turf, too. I had to be purposeful in spending time with them. Generally, I did a good job of that, but I made mistakes. Once, back in 1977, I had somehow landed tickets to an NBA Finals game between the Portland Trailblazers and the Philadelphia 76ers. The game was on Sunday afternoon. I was going to go watch it with my son, Todd. However, I was scheduled to preach the day of the game, and instead of handing over the sermon duties to someone else, I handed over the tickets instead. I chose being a pastor over being a dad, and I missed out on what would have been an unforgettable afternoon with my son.

I regretted that decision for years, and made a commitment that I would never miss out on important activities with my kids. That was a tall order. Kim, Todd, and Ryan were all very active, and they had broad interests. They played sports, they played instruments, they sang, they did drama. They kept us moving all through the 70's, 80's and early 90's. But Lynna Gay and I loved the pace, and we did our absolute best to make it to every game, every recital, every concert, and every event of importance. And we were successful in that effort, excluding the rarest of exceptions.

Our family grew so close, in large part to that commitment. We loved each other. Kim and Todd had grown up, and Ryan was in high school. Kim had long since married a wonderful young man named Levi, and the two of them were leading worship for the church—Levi on the keyboard, and Kim on the mic. They were a powerful duo, and I loved having them as a part of our ministry. Todd and Ryan were full of energy and passion for life, for God, and for us.

Lynna Gay and I weren't perfect parents by any means, and we weren't a perfect couple, either. We made plenty of mistakes. But as I lay in that hospital bed, pondering whether or not my house was in order, I was filled with gratitude. I didn't want to die, but I wasn't afraid of dying, either, because I had none of those crushing familial regrets that so many men find waiting for them on their deathbeds. I was confident in our family's love. And if I went home to my Savior that day, I could go, knowing I had been a good father.

My house was, indeed, in order.

When I was confident of that answer, I turned my attention inward. Did I have personal regrets about my other life's work? About my ministry as a pastor? Had I been faithful with the gifts God had given me? I thought of the parable of the talents, and asked God, assuming He had given me ten talents, how many of them I had invested.

The answer was as clear as it was painful. "You've used three talents," He said.

Just three.

But the memories were good and strong. Hadn't I obeyed God when He called me? Hadn't I started the church out of obedience? Hadn't I preached with boldness? Hadn't I loved the church? Hadn't I won souls and rallied God's people to do the same?

Three talents? That's it?

Then, His whisper came to me: "You were afraid to take risks. You were afraid to fail."

If anyone else had accused me so, I would have bristled. But this was God speaking. I knew His voice. And when the words came, I knew the truth in them. I remembered all the times God had called me to step out and I had refused. I saw myself walking past the world map in our hallway, ignoring the scary call of heaven, "Ask of me, and I will give you nations as your inheritance." Psalm 2:8 NKJV

Had I ever been as bold as I had pretended to be? No. Not really. On the outside, I had been brave. But God doesn't look on the outside.

Thus, for the third time that season, a lurking and ugly truth pushed through my facade to humble me. First the church split. Then the heart attack. And now, on the heels of that heart attack, came this: the revelation that I had pulled punches, that I was not the cavalier minister God had called me to be, that I had often stepped back when He had summoned me forward.

"I had more for you, but you were afraid." God said.

There was no anger in His voice, however. It was a rebuke, yes, but it was laced with gentleness. I knew God loved me. I knew that if I died, I would be with Him in His presence for all time.

Still, the revelation stung. I had fancied myself a risk taker, and in comparison to others, maybe I was. But God doesn't waste time comparing us to others. He simply calls us to obey.

Sometimes, our lack of obedience is, at root, a fear that God isn't as good as He promised to be. Sometimes we get scared that

He won't hold up His end of the bargain. I thought of the church split. I thought of how the entire episode could have been avoided by a simple, personal act of obedience more than ten years earlier. God had spoken to me way back then, and I had disobeyed out of simple, ugly fear.

"Lord, I'm sorry," I prayed. "You're right. I was afraid! Forgive me, please!"

And then, staring up at the ceiling before I went under, I promised God I wouldn't make that mistake again. I told Him if I lived through that operation that I would take risks when He called me to. I promised not to back down. From then on, I would believe the Holy Spirit when He called me. I would step out and look like a fool. I would pray bigger prayers, and take bigger risks. I would, to the best of my ability, use all my talents.

Soon, the anesthesia started taking effect, and world around me dimmed. When I woke up, life would never be the same.

Part 2

Chapter 9: Harlem

My hospital bed promise to God was like a soldier's prayer in a foxhole: "Lord if you get me out of this, I'll serve you forever." Such prayers are easily forgotten when the breakthrough comes. But my vow to take bigger risks for Jesus didn't fall away after my surgery. If anything, it intensified.

I recovered from my quadruple bypass, and was soon back on my feet. The outreaches continued, as did our conviction that God was doing something unique with our congregation in regards to outreaches. He was continuing to call us out.

As we began planning our spring break outreach in 1994, we prayed and asked God where we should go. I felt like God said, "Harlem."

As a destination, New York City was less than ideal. For some parents, it was just about the scariest location on earth. Back then, the Big Apple was not the attractive tourist destination it is today. According to the official New York City government statistics, in 1990 alone, there were 2,262 reported murders, over 3,000 reported rapes, and more than 122,000 burglaries! Those numbers have taken a dramatic nosedive in subsequent decades, thanks be to God

We had already taken a team to New York in our flurry of outreaches, but this was different. Harlem was one of the most depressed and crime ridden areas in all New York. It was not the place it is today. At the time, the leading cause of death in that neighborhood was homicide.

"Guys, I heard Harlem," I told my elders. And in the end, they agreed.

We had contacts in New Jersey, but I didn't want to commute. I wanted to stay in Harlem itself. So I called the chamber of commerce and asked for some names of churches there. That was the way outreach teams often found housing, they would call a church in search of an auditorium floor or an empty classroom to throw their sleeping bags on. Of course, this was well before the days of cell phones and quick Google searches. Back then, we had to do actual research before we went places.

The lady I spoke with gave me the names of three churches in Harlem that we could call. I struck out on the first two, but on my third try, I talked to a man named Gordon Williams, one of the pastors at Bethel Gospel Assembly. Bethel was a large African-American church with a long, storied history in Harlem.

"You want to do what?" he asked, incredulous.

I told him I wanted to take our high school kids to Harlem so they could paint their faces white and do the mime drama Zion all over the city. It must have sounded insane to Pastor Gordon. In addition to the obvious crime concerns that all country folk like us had, there was also the racial tension to deal with. Harlem was overwhelmingly African-American, and the city has a long, troubled history in regards to race. Still, I asked if him if his church would do us the honor of hosting us on our little adventure.

He laughed. "If you're crazy enough to bring a bunch of white kids to Harlem, I can be crazy enough to let you sleep on our gym floor."

It was the beginning of a wonderful and wholly unlikely partnership.

New York City probably seemed just as foreign to our kids as Mexico had. Manhattan's towering skyscrapers and suffocating traffic were marvels. It's overwhelming numbers were on full kinetic display in the crosswalks. It was a far cry from Junction City, Oregon, population 6,182.

Bethel Gospel Assembly was situated right in the heart of East Harlem. We stayed on the floor of the church's two gymnasiums, girls in one, and boys in the other. Our hosts let us use their kitchen, and the building served as a base of operations. I stayed with the boys in the gym, despite the protests of the church leadership, who urged me to stay with one of their host homes. It was important, in my mind, to not have separation between the students and the leaders.

When we went out to minister, we caused a scene, let me tell you. Imagine a horde of white mimes running around Harlem doing dramas to loud music. We were a sight to see! Even when we were just crossing the street, people stopped and gaped.

The fact that we looked so out of place helped us, though. When we set up our portable sound system in parks, the crowds came to watch whatever was going to happen. They couldn't believe what they were seeing. We did one performance on Martin Luther King Boulevard, and caused a traffic jam.

Our itinerary was loose. We would ask God where we should go, then we would go there and set up. One afternoon, I had to go into a barbershop holding the cord to our soundboard. I asked the owner of the place if he would let us plug in so we could run our program. The man said yes, and I thanked him, but I also warned him we were about to shut him down for a good half hour. We did.

Before going on, I should tell you a little bit more about Zion, the mime drama we performed those years, because it was easily the best tool for sharing the gospel we ever used. That might sound funny to modern ears. Like any tool, this one had a shelf life. Mimes don't work very well anymore in the U.S., but back then, they were quite effective in open air settings.

The story begins with a character representing Jesus. Optimistic music plays while He creates the world, and He creates a daughter, Zion. He embraces her, shows her His world, and gives her a white handkerchief—the symbol of a pure heart. And it is clear to the audience—*this is the way it is supposed to be.*

But of course it can't last. Another character, Satan, enters in. He can't steal her handkerchief directly, so he resorts to other means. He brings in a series of other characters representing various entrapments for the human heart. One is materialism—a person who gets Zion focused entirely on herself and her own appearance. It works, and an exchange is made. Zion now has a colored handkerchief.

It gets worse after that. She gets tricked by temptation after temptation—characters representing lust, drugs, alcohol, the occult—and all the while, Jesus is watching her from the back of the stage. He's calling out to her, but she can't hear Him. And in the end, poor Zion is left with nothing but a black handkerchief.

She is ruined, and she knows it. And the audience can see what has happened. *It was never supposed to be this way.*

Sensing his opportunity, Satan reemerges and crucifies Jesus. Then, he moves in to kill Zion. The audience would be into it at this point. Scandalized, even! Why was he killing such a loving character? But of course, Jesus doesn't stay dead. He comes back to life to save His daughter in the eleventh hour, vanquishes the devil, and exchanges Zion's black handkerchief with a fresh white one. The drama ends there, with restored relationship and a heart made new by the risen Christ.

When people watched this drama, they would relate to Zion's brokenness. They would become invested in her, and would feel terrible when things went south. Once, we even had someone jump on stage and try to protect her from Satan! The reason for such reactions was obvious, they saw themselves in her both her sin and her desperation. When I would come on stage after that and invite people to have their own hearts made new, they responded. They knew they needed that new heart as badly as she had.

In Harlem, the response to Zion was awesome. Many people were struck in particular by the drug and alcohol temptations, since those things had so ravaged the community. "I want to meet Jesus," audience members would call out. And I would send the students out to pray for them. These were often rough characters. We had drug dealers and prostitutes weeping with the revolutionary love of Christ. And hundreds of people said yes to the gospel.

When we weren't doing Zion, we were building relationships with the people of that community. We brought our basketball team with us, and they found some pickup games at the local playgrounds. And they held their own. Our boys were always good. Surprisingly good. It was wonderful to watch them mix together with the local young people. They had a great time.

Of all that happened on that outreach, though, one event stands out more than all the others. It was the day we did Zion for an entire public school.

We had the kids in vans, and we had asked God where we should go. We wound up in front of an inner-city elementary school. I had the kids wait in the vans with the other adults, and I stepped into the office.

The principal was an African-American woman who clearly cared for her students. She cared about them getting an education. I knew that at once, because she flat out turned me down when I asked her if we could pull them all out of classes to watch our drama.

"Mr. Bowers, we can't stop the entire school day just for you."

Of course she couldn't. It was an unreasonable request. An arrogant one, even! But I knew it was God. I knew He was impressing this on me. And I knew that when He spoke, I had to obey. This was one of those risks I had promised Him I wouldn't shrink back from.

So I leaned in and said something like this, "Ma'am, we go where God tells us. And when we do, nobody turns us down."

She turned us down.

Still, I wasn't ready to give up just yet. "You see them?" I said, pointing out the window at the two vans parked outside. "Those vans are full of kids in face paint, ready to put on this drama."

At that, she sighed in surrender, and said something along the lines of what Pastor Gordon had said, "If you've got enough guts to bring a bunch of white kids here, I guess I can have the guts to put them onstage."

I went out to tell the students, and the principal sprang into action. She made an announcement that there would be an impromptu assembly, and all classes were to report to the auditorium. When they all arrived, there were 750 of them staring at us. Not a single white face in their midst. Once again, we were a spectacle!

The principal introduced us, and our kids took their places. For the next fifteen minutes, they performed Zion, and the students were transfixed. By the end of it, the principal had tears streaming down her face.

"This was a gift from God." she said to me, shaking her head. "What are we supposed to do now? We can't just leave it here!"

In any other environment, we would have given the altar call, "Who here wants to receive Jesus?" But this was a public school.

That kind of thing was very much against the rules. We were toeing the line already. The only reason we could get away with doing the drama at all was because it had no words to it, and was open to interpretation.

But the principal was right. We couldn't just leave it there. The kids had questions.

"I have twenty-three students who would love to talk to the kids directly. Can I let them?"

She nodded, and I released our students into the crowd. The kids in the audience mobbed them. They wanted to talk. They wanted to ask questions. They wanted to make friends. And once that began, we couldn't stop it.

The principal watched it all with wonder. There was something so hope-filled about the scene, and she was clearly moved. "This is one of the most amazing days I've ever had in this school," she said. "God came along and gave this gift to me!" Then she invited us to spend the rest of the day with the students. We did. I'll never forget it.

By the end of the outreach, we had shared the gospel with thousands of people. We would often hand out response cards to those who gave their lives to Jesus. People would write their name, address, and phone number on those cards so that a local church could get in touch with them. Obviously, since we lived in Oregon, we couldn't disciple any new converts in New York City. So we gave all those cards to our host pastors at Bethel Gospel Assembly. I don't remember exactly how many of them, but there were at least 250.

The best part of that trip, though, besides all the souls that came into the kingdom, was the relationship that began. I had spent some time that week with Pastor Gordon and another pastor, Carl Phipps, and I liked them. We had much in common. We loved the Lord, we loved His people, and we loved the nations.

And yet, we couldn't have been more different, either. These men had grown up on the receiving end of all kinds of racial injustice in the heart of the city, while I was a well-to-do farmer's son in white, rural Oregon. Their church was large and well-known, but nobody had ever heard of Christ's Center, or the town it was in.

All the same, I felt something unique, and I told them so. "Let's start a relationship between our churches," I said. They must have felt it, too, because even though it didn't make much sense, they agreed. I had not yet met the top leader of their church—a Bishop named Ezra Williams—but I was getting to know these two, and that was enough for me.

The two of them flew out to Oregon to visit us after we returned home. And while they were there, we sensed the Lord confirming His word: Bethel Gospel Assembly and Christ's Center were tied together in some divinely appointed brotherhood. We had all watched Jesus heal the wounds of Zion and give her hope again; we knew He could heal the wounds between races and cultures, too. And now we had an open door.

All that was left was to meet the Bishop.

Chapter 10: The Bishop

One week after they left Oregon for their Harlem home, Pastor Gordon called me with an urgent invitation. Bethel Gospel Assembly was about to have their annual missions conference in Harlem, he said, and I was invited. The Bishop wanted me to come. And he didn't just want me to attend. No, he wanted to have me speak at the conference.

"Jon, this is really big," Pastor Gordon said. "We have never had a white man come up and speak from that platform. This is a big deal. Don't say no." I didn't say no. Instead, Lynna Gay and I flew into Harlem to meet the legendary man we had heard so much about.

Bishop Ezra Nehemiah Williams was thirteen years older than me. He was a slight man in stature, but there was nothing small about him. No truly small man can carry an entire community on his shoulders the way he did.

As a boy, young Ezra lived in a cruel era. Harlem was an impoverished community suffering under the weight of segregation and bitter prejudice. Ezra himself was on the receiving end both of racism and ridicule. The odds were stacked against him. In school, he was particularly troubled. Teachers sent sending him to the principal's office so often that the principal finally threw up his hands and told Ezra he would never amount to anything but a loser.

Thankfully, Ezra ignored such prognostications. He grew into a hard worker, serving in the U.S. Army, and taking a job driving public busses around the city. Every day when his shift was over, he would have to ride another bus to get home, and he had to sit in the back due to the color of his skin.

Eventually, he found his way into ministry, where he became a powerful Pentecostal preacher. In the early 1980's, as pastor of Bethel Gospel Assembly, he directed the church to purchase the old junior high school building in East Harlem. The property took up an entire city block. After a long season of renovation, the church made that building their new home, and Ezra installed his own pastoral office in the exact spot where the former principal's office used to be—the very same principal who had condemned him to a life of mediocrity. It was a holy irony.

"The Bish," as his parishioners often called him, told that story often from the pulpit. It was a testament to God's redemptive power even in bleak circumstances. It is no surprise that the church grew so large under his leadership, or that he became so renown for bringing hope to the oppressed and downtrodden.

When I finally met the man himself, before his missions conference in 1994, I saw how sincere his smile was. The Bishop was always full of warmth. It was obvious that he loved people. But I could tell he was conflicted, too. He wasn't against the notion that our two churches might be friends, exactly, but he was hesitant. And he had good reason for hesitation.

"Jon, I have a problem." he said as we sat down to get acquainted. "Half my leaders don't want me to put you on that platform."

I shrugged. "That's okay, I don't need to speak. I can sit up and watch the service from the balcony."

But he shook his head. "No. Because the other half of my leaders do want you up there."

"So, what do you want to do, Bishop?" I asked.

He sighed, letting the weight sink down on his shoulders. "I don't know."

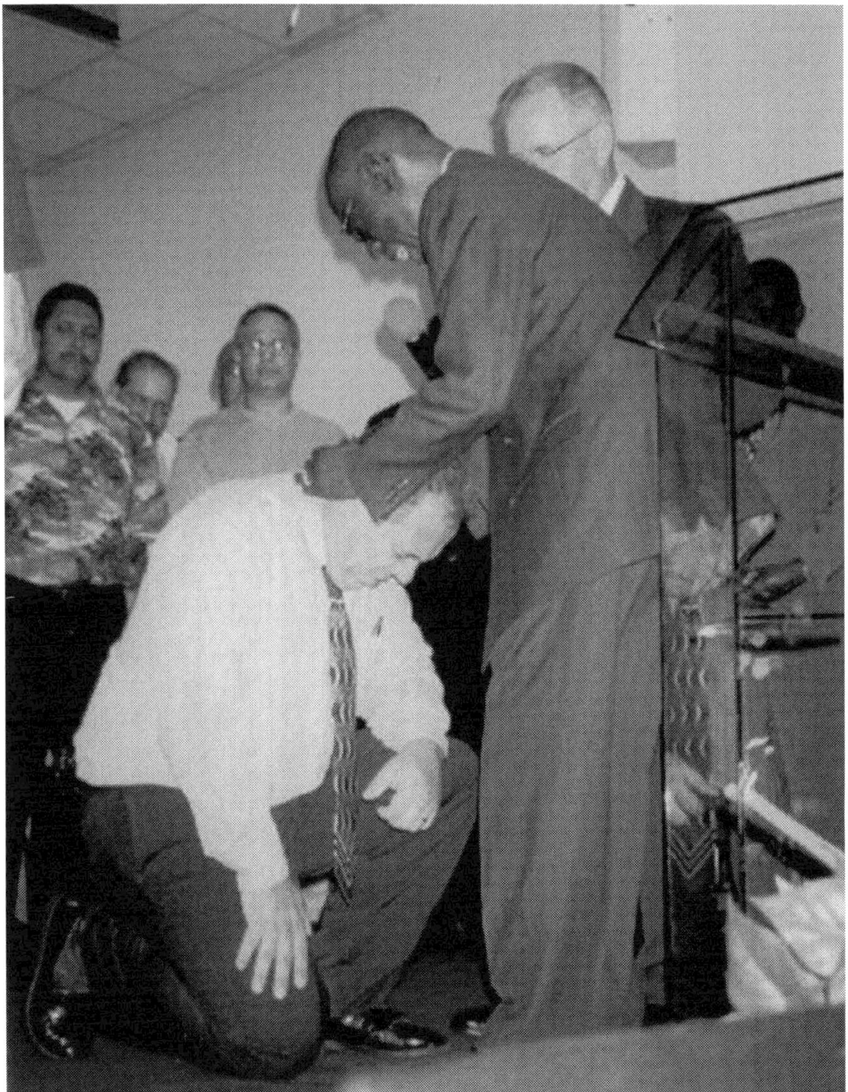

Bishop Ezra Williams of Harlem New York praying over Pastor Alijhandro during the Cuban 2004 pastor conference. Pastor Jon is next to the Bishop.

Then he told me one of his leaders had promised to walk out of the church and never come back if he let "that white pastor" speak. I had no intention of rocking the boat. I had only just met this man, and I didn't want to put him in such a tight spot.

"Wouldn't it be easier if we just called this off? I'll just leave town," I said.

But the Bishop shook his head. "No, Jon. No. I believe this is God. But I'll be honest…I'm very concerned."

I was concerned, too. Not only for my new friends, but for me. I didn't ask to be put in this hotbed of controversy. I had simply accepted an invitation!

That night, I made my own decision. I told Lynna Gay that I wasn't going to speak. It was too risky. Things could get out of hand really quickly. We would leave town.

When she heard me say that, she turned and faced me. "Jon Bowers," she said. "Since when do you back down from a challenge?"

So the day of the conference came, and the auditorium was packed. There was a bit of a circus environment. Word had gotten out about the white pastor that was going to share, and the crowds came flocking in to see what was going to happen.

At last, the moment came, and Bishop Ezra Williams introduced me. I walked out onto stage, and it was silent.

Now, you must understand: Bethel Gospel Assembly is anything but silent and stoic. They are a Pentecostal church, full of "amens" and "hallelujahs." Tourist buses make special stops there so travelers can experience first hand the beauty and excitement of authentic gospel music. The church even had a welcome song that the whole congregation would sing to first time visitors. In short, these folks know how to let their exuberance shine before men. But on that morning, when I was introduced, there were no cheers. No claps. Nothing but crickets.

I had a specific message to preach to them, but earlier that morning, I felt like the Holy Spirit was leading me to do something else entirely.

I motioned to a lady in the congregation to carry up the basin of water she had just prepared for me. Then, I called the Bishop on stage and asked him to sit in the chair, and I knelt at his feet.

People began to gasp. In that church culture, nobody touches the Bishop. He's a man of too much honor. And here I was, a clueless white man, rolling up this man's pant legs and taking his shoes off.

"I wish I could wash all your feet this morning," I told the mass of stunned faces, "but this will have to do."

The washing of feet was a special, intimate kind of service in Jesus' day. It was the kind of thing the lowliest servant might do for an honored traveler. On the night Jesus was betrayed, he took a basin to all of his disciples and washed their feet. He became the servant of all.

Nowadays, with our shoes and socks and our daily habits of hygiene, we don't generally need to perform this duty. Nevertheless, something powerful happens when we emulate Jesus' act in Jesus' way. It signals humility and esteem. It tells the person: "I honor you above myself." Such an act never fails to leave a deep impression.

That morning was no different. As I was washing the Bishop's feet, I heard him sniffle. I looked up in his eyes, and he was crying.

The Spirit of God fell. All around the congregation, God was working. He was breaking down barriers I didn't even understand. I didn't have to overcome decades of hurt and injustice to be here. I simply got on a plane and obeyed. For me, this was a little thing. But God wasn't doing a little thing here. He was doing a deep healing work that began in this man whose feet I held in my hands—a bold man who had taken a massive risk.

By the time I was done, people all around the congregation were crying. I dried the bishop's feet, and was already stepping off the stage to be finished. He stopped me, though, and said, "Now I want to wash your feet."

So I sat down, took my shoes off, and watched this powerful saint get on his knees in front of me. His face was full of the love of the Holy Spirit. The audience was in awe of what they were seeing. The walls continued to crumble.

As I sunk my feet into the water, I suddenly remembered that I had an infected toe. I didn't want to tell him just then due to the solemn nature of the moment, but when the Bishop touched my toe, I started to shake. It stung so badly!

"Thank you, Jesus!" The bishop said, and squeezed my toe again, and my body shook harder. Pain shot through my leg, but his eyes were squeezed shut in fervent prayer, and he wouldn't let go. I was trying not to let it show on my face, but it was excruciating! After the service I explained to him about the stinging pain, and he began to laugh. "I thought you were just being moved by Holy Spirit!"

When my feet were dry and my shoes were back on my feet, the bishop took the microphone again and addressed the crowd.

"Now Saints at Bethel, I want to introduce our speaker again," he said. "This is Pastor Jon Bowers of Christ's Center Church in Oregon!"

We embraced, and this time, the room exploded in raucous applause. I'm telling you, the roof just came off the place! It was an unforgettable moment that sealed not only the relationship between Bethel Gospel Assembly and Christ's Center Church, but also between Ezra Nehemiah Williams and Jon Bowers.

That relationship was one of the most significant of my adult life. The Bishop would fly into town and stay in my guest bedroom. We would fellowship over the breakfast table, or over his dinner table in New York. We went rafting down the McKenzie River; we would go to Yankee games. He would stand at my pulpit, and I would stand in his. And we would talk late into the evenings, trading wisdom about God, life, and ministry.

This wasn't an experiment in cross-cultural, racial reconciliation. It was simple friendship. Simple, beautiful, God-ordained friendship.

It's easy to overcomplicate such matters in today's world. The Bishop knew that better than anyone else. Being such a stalwart figure in such a historic church, he was always being called on for high profile, cross-cultural meetings. Those meetings often happened in white churches with pastors looking to demonstrate diversity and racial healing. He had grown exhausted by such efforts. Truly, when we first met, he had little interest in pursuing racial reconciliation at all. He had been burned too many times before.

The Bishop told me about one such event. It happened long after we had become friends. A group of white pastors in the city had called and asked him in to speak at their event on racial reconciliation. They accepted the invitation, and when it was his turn to preach, he got up and only spoke for a moment. He told them all about his pastor friend in Oregon who had invited him into his home. He told them of how the two of us ate at one another's supper tables, and shared life.

Then he turned to those who had invited him, and he didn't mince words. They had never invited him into their homes. They had never eaten together. They had never shown any interest in his friendship. They only tried to use him.

He shook his head, and stepped down off the stage. He was finished.

Years later, I called my friend and invited him to make another trip to Oregon. He said he couldn't come. I asked him why, and he explained that he was having some health problems that caused him to bleed at night. If he came to stay in my guest room, he would soil my sheets, he said, and he didn't want to do that.

I confess, I got a little upset with him. "You listen here," I told him. "I want you to fly to Oregon. I want you to come to my house. You are my friend, and I want you to come bleed on my sheets."

He relented. My friend came to my house and slept in my guest room. I considered it a great honor.

I don't tell those two stories to brag on myself, but to brag on my friend Ezra Williams. He was the one baring the scars of racial injustice. He was the one who had been hurt by white men his whole life—including a whole herd of white pastors. He was the one who had taken the risk in order to embrace a man he had only just met, and God richly rewarded both of us for his boldness.

The Bishop was, in short, living the kind of life I was aspiring to live—a full-bore, ten-talent, risky-obedience kind of life. His decision to listen and open his heart to us had vast repercussions. The bond that formed between the two of us and our churches became the foundational stone of something God was already forming, a most unlikely Alliance that would stretch across the nations.

Chapter 11: Guatemala

"Ask of me and I will give you nations," the verse went. In the early months and years after my heart attack, when I was committed to investing my talents, I heard that challenge in my heart, His voice in my spirit. God had already been stretching me. Our adventure with Harlem, and our various mission ventures had done a good job of that. The further we went, the more flexible we became. Obedience was becoming more routine. That was a good thing.

Still, though I had never really accepted the "ask of me" challenge of Psalm 2. Whenever I walked by the world map in the hallway, it would still call out to me. But what would I do with a nation? Who was I to hold that kind of influence, whatever it entailed?

Finally, in 1994, I gave in. It was partly out of obedience, and partly out of exhaustion. I wanted to get the ringing out of my ears, so I told God, "Fine, Lord. Give me this nation right here." And with closed eyes, I pointed blindly to the map, and found my finger was touching Central America; specifically, the nation of Guatemala.

"Okay, Lord. Give me Guatemala."

God started our work in Guatemala but not with Jon Bowers. He would use another man. An unlikely servant.

Now, I had long ago learned that God could use anyone to do big things. He had used me, for one, even though I had never spent a day in Bible school. I was a farmer and a teacher, but there He was, turning me into a minister of the gospel. And I watched him do the same thing with men like Tom Crabb, Michael O'Barr, and Bishop Williams. All of us had been passed over by the world only to be exalted by our heavenly father. All of us saw our Lord work mightily through us, despite our weaknesses, our disadvantages, and our past failures. But none of us was less likely to do great things in the kingdom than my friend Herb Christensen.

Herb was one of the more colorful men I've ever known. For most of his adult life, he had been an addict. Drugs alcohol pulled him down over and over again. But he was also a bold and unflinching trailblazer. I knew God had something in store for this man, so I began to take him under my wing, even during his relapses. And he had many relapses. I watched them up close. He put his wife and kids on an emotional roller coaster for years as he destroyed his body with chemicals.

Finally, after three open-heart surgeries, when even his old drinking buddies tried to steer him away from his old lifestyle, Herb got a call from a friend named Linda. Linda was taking a private plane on a missions trip through Central America. Her plan was to land at various airports and disperse thousands of Spanish-language gospel tracts, and she wanted Herb to help her.

So he came to me with the opportunity and asked me what I thought. The fact that Guatemala was in Central America was not lost on me. Could this be the beginning of God's answer?

We prayed about it that day, and I felt like God was in it, despite Herb's continued weakness. I had found that outreaches could do a world of good for people struggling through the sanctification process. God has a way of meeting people on the mission field, and I don't mean the natives. He meets those who go. Herb was weak, to be sure, but God shows himself strong to those who need Him the most.

Thus, Herb and his teenage son, Mark, stepped onto a small, twin engine plane bound for Central and South America. As the plane passed over the Gulf of Mexico, they noticed the engine was smoking. If they could have, they would have turned back to New Orleans, where they took off, but they were already past the point of no return. They would have to make an emergency landing in Belize. It was the first sign that this trip was not going to go according to plan.

Or was it? “A man’s heart plans his way,” Proverbs 16:9 tells us, “But the Lord directs his steps.” No matter what we have in mind, God is never boring. He loves to surprise us, especially when we are about His business.

The team managed to land safely in Belize to get their engine fixed, and ended up in Guatemala City. There they bummed around the airport for an entire afternoon, trying to get ahold of some missionary in the country who might host them for a few days.

After they had wasted hours on the phone, a suspicious looking American approached them. His eyes were angry, and he wore a gun on his hip. “Who are you people?” he barked.

They told him, “We are missionaries.” He was not happy with that answer. He told them to stay put in the airport restaurant until he gave them further orders.

They waited hours for him, not daring to disobey. When he came back, he ushered them into a small minivan, gun still on his hip.

“I’m with the CIA,” he told them once they got inside. “And I was investigating an active bomb threat on the airport.” See what I mean? Following God is never boring!

The man went on to tell them how he hated missionaries, because missionaries were always coming down there to scam the good people of Guatemala, living off the land and pretending to be altruistic. He didn't believe in God, and he didn't believe in God's people. There was only one missionary in the whole country that he respected, and that was where he was taking them.

"His name is Ronny Coffer," he said.

Ronny Coffer was a man of grace and influence. He and his wife were the directors of "Ministries of His Glory." They hosted all sorts of missionary and medical relief teams in their compound, complete with a kitchen, dorms, and full bedding. More important than his resources, however, was the incredible favor on his life. Not only did the CIA trust him implicitly, the Guatemalans did, too.

When Herb met Ronny, he knew at once this was why God had sent him on that trip. His scouting mission had been a radical success. Yes, they had almost wound up in a plane crash, and yes, they had been accosted by a CIA agent in the middle of a bomb threat, but none of that mattered. He had found the man God had sent him there to meet.

When Herb reported the story to me, I knew his assessment was correct. Ronny was our man, and I knew this was God's colorful way of answering my request for the nation of Guatemala.

Before Ronny realized what he was getting into, he was hosting a Zion team from Christ's Center. I was there with them. We followed the same kind of loose schedule as we had in Tijuana. We drove around the city until we found a place to do Zion—usually it was a park. Then, we would pray, share the gospel in the drama and in word. At the end of the day, we would reconvene at our base, with a time of worship and a recap of what God had done that day. We called that "Upper Room" time, and we cherished those hours. God was moving, just like He had in Mexico, and we were full of faith.

Then, one afternoon, as we drove back to Ronny's compound, we passed a large closed gate with soldiers inside. It was a military base.

"Let's stop in here and see if we can do Zion for the soldiers," I said.

Ronny frowned. It was a ludicrous idea and we both knew it. A military base was hardly a good environment for young teenagers even in good times, but these were not good times for Guatemala. The country was in the middle of a civil war.

"Let's go talk to the general," I said.

"Jon, we can't just go talk to the general and ask to do a drama!"

And of course, he was right. You can't just go do things like that. But I wasn't about to let that stop me. I knew God was in this.

"Ronny, I think God is asking us to minister to these soldiers," I said.

Ronny shook his head. "Fine, you and Ciro can take my jeep up the mountain to go talk to them, but I'm staying here."

Ciro Gutierrez was my translator. He was another one of those unlikely heroes of the kingdom, having been a nightclub owner and pimp (among other things) before God took hold of his life. Since then, he had become an unstoppable force for the sharing of the Gospel, and a dear friend. When Ciro and I are together, everyone hears about Jesus. Everyone. Even soldiers.

"Hi, we'd like to do a drama for your men." Ciro told the guard in Spanish. A crowd of soldiers gathered around. Rather than turning us away, they opened up a gate and gave us a ride to the general's office. It was unheard of!

We marched into the general's office unannounced, and the secretary let us in to see him. We exchanged pleasantries and told him what we'd told the other soldiers, we had a drama to show him and his men.

"What's the drama about?" he asked.

We told him it was about Jesus and His love for us, and how if we accepted Him, we could go to heaven.

"I'll tell you what," he said in Spanish. "You be here at 6:00 tonight for the lowering of our flag, and I'll have a few soldiers here to watch the drama."

We went back down the mountain and told Ronnie. His jaw hit the floor.

"Are you kidding me? You got into the base? Nobody has ever gotten in there before!" I smiled. It wasn't me. It was God at work. Clearly.

The team got ready and piled back into the two vans, and together, we drove back up the mountain. The soldiers at the gate let us through without any trouble this time. I can't imagine what they must have been thinking, letting two vans full of white American kids in mime makeup.

We set up the sound system on a platform beneath the flagpoles and waited. Then, we heard them. Drums. Chants. Feet stomping in perfect unison. A huge block of soldiers marched in tight formation, falling in line in front of the flagpoles. Somebody started counting. Three hundred. Then, more drums. Another block. Then another. By the time they were all assembled, there were six hundred and thirty soldiers.

We stood quietly, feeling excited and a little overwhelmed, while they carefully lowered the flag. A translator stood next to me, quietly explaining what was happening with each step of the ceremony. When the flag was down, the general told the soldiers to sit on the ground. He invited me to the front and gave me the floor.

"We're going to tell you about Jesus this evening," Ciro and I told them. And I signaled to the kids to begin. I have to give it to these kids. They must have been nervous, thousands of miles from home in a country torn by civil war, and now surrounded by six hundred and thirty soldiers. I had told them what the general told me… that there would be "a FEW soldiers."

But nerves or no nerves, the music began, and our kids performed beautifully the drama of sin and redemption through Jesus. And when it was over, I stood up and took the microphone, as was my custom. I asked them who wanted to accept Jesus; who wanted to follow Zion's lead by exchanging their darkened hearts for a new one white as snow.

A line of commanders was the first to respond. They stood to their feet indicating that yes, they wanted Jesus. Then, many more. Men all over the company stood to their feet and raised their hands. They also wanted a new heart. In the end, a large percentage of that crowd—literally hundreds of them—were on their feet inviting Jesus into their lives.

Ciro and I led them all in the sinner's prayer. But I sensed it wasn't over. There was more. "How many of you need prayer for family members?" I asked the crowd. Again, hundreds of hands went up. I turned to our team. "Okay, kids, quick prayers." And I sent them out into the mass of foreign soldiers. It didn't matter that they couldn't speak the language. They went anyway, lightly laying hands on the shoulders of these strange, threatening men, asking God to shine His light on their loved ones.

The general was impressed. Very impressed. When it was over he called me to his office and said, "This is without a doubt a move of God." Then he picked up the phone and called a general of another military base. This one was on the coast. He spoke for a moment in Spanish then turned to us. "Can you be at this base tomorrow morning at ten-thirty?"

"Yes," I said without hesitation.

He confirmed the plans and hung up the phone. "Our soldiers all over Guatemala need to see this drama." he said.

We went to the next base the following morning, and just as he promised, there was another large group of soldiers ready to watch and receive. Three hundred and thirty of them, this time. We put on the drama, and once again, a massive number of men stood up to receive a new heart from Jesus. I don't know how many of them did, but it was the majority. After we had prayed, and the soldiers were dismissed, the general's wife came to me with tears in her eyes.

"I saw this in a dream!" She exclaimed. "This is what our soldiers need. You must go to every military base in Guatemala and do this drama!"

They sent me to a third base. This time, there were two hundred and twenty soldiers. We did Zion for these men, and again, a majority of them responded by inviting Jesus into their lives. That general pulled me aside afterward. "I've talked to the other two generals who have seen this," he told me through Ciro. "And we're all in agreement. You need to go meet John Rivieta, the head of the army. He is in charge of the entire army. And when you meet him, he will insist that you go to every military base in the country."

And at that, I thought back to something the general had told me: "If you stay focused on the military, you will own this country." Now they were all saying it in different ways.

"Ask of me," the Lord whispered again. It was like a warm smile inside me; a holy poke in the ribs that meant, "I told you so. And just you wait and see what happens next."

Chapter 12: The General

General John Rivieta was a powerful man. As head of the armed forces throughout the nation, his offices were in the heart of Guatemala City. The other generals had helped to get me an appointment with him, but it was more than that. God had an appointment with Him.

We drove to the city in our vans. The students were already in their costumes and face paint even though they were not invited to this meeting. Whatever happened, I wanted them to be ready. We pulled up to "The White House", as they called it, though it was neither white nor a house. It was a rather imposing military compound surrounded by a high wall, and it was gray in color. The soldiers opened the gate for us and we drove between buildings. In the center of them, all was a wide grass courtyard, and there were armed guards all around.

Everything about the setting was intimidating. I had no business being there. I was just a farmer from Oregon after all! But oddly enough, I wasn't nervous because I knew I wasn't setting any of this up. This was God's mission, not my own.

One of the guards led Ciro and me inside one of the buildings, and soon enough, we were standing in front of General John Rivieta, the head of the Guatemalan military and the second most powerful man in the country. I was immediately struck by his pristine white uniform and his perfect English.

We exchanged pleasantries, and he told us he had spent time

studying in New Hampshire. He was gracious at first as he told me about his conversations with the other generals.

"They are excited about this drama you have." he said. "And it's very interesting. Thank you for coming. Next time you are in Guatemala, please let us know. I would love to have coffee with you."

I grunted. There would probably be a next time, Lord willing, but I wasn't about to wait until then. This appointment was too important. God had the momentum now, and I didn't want to stand in His way. So I pressed forward.

"With all due respect, sir," I said, "we didn't come all this way just so we could greet one another. We came to show you the drama that has shaken up these bases."

He shook his head. He was clearly distracted and not in the mood to haggle. "I don't have time to see the drama. I have the agricultural minister of Denmark here to see me, and he's waiting for me right now."

Again, I took a risk.

"Sir, I'm not leaving until we show you the drama."

It was the first time I had ever talked back to the military commander of a foreign power. It's not necessarily something I would recommend. But again, God was in it, and I knew it. "This is about a move of God that has already swept through three of your bases. I have the kids in the vans outside right now. They're ready."

The generals' pleasantness vanished now. He was getting irritated.

"Well, how long would it take?"

"Only fifteen minutes," I said.

"And where would you do it?"

"We could do it right here in this office."

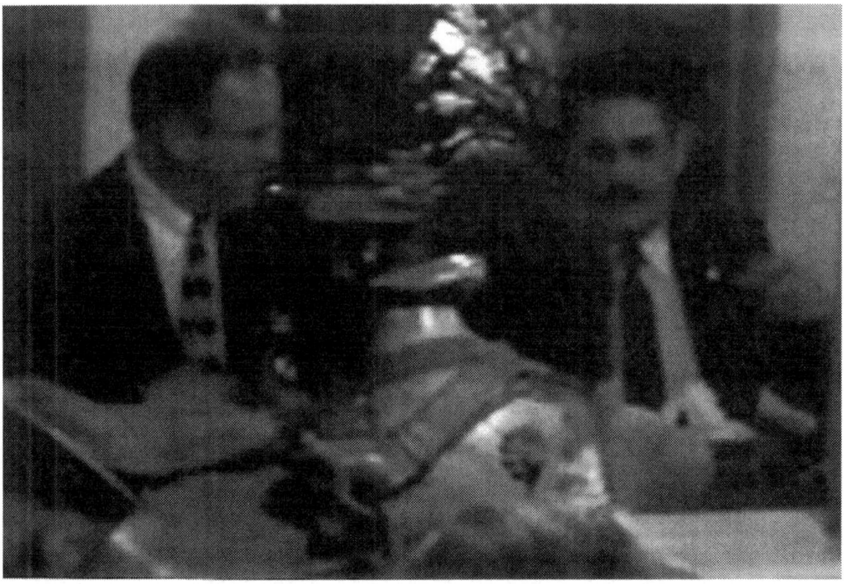

Jon and General Riveta

"Fine." he said. And with that, he barked a few orders before stepping out of the room to collect himself. I ran out to the van to pull in our students. It would be the most important performance they had ever given.

So there we were, a collection of white Americans—mostly high school students in mime makeup—squished together in a government compound, surrounded by the military leaders for an entire nation. There were nine other officers present, and I sat next to General Rivieta himself.

The music started, and the kids sprung into action. They were likely nervous, but once the drama began, they told the story of sin and redemption through Jesus just like it was any other performance. They didn't see what I saw, though, General Rivieta looked angry. Furious, even.

I determined that as soon as it was over, I would get those kids out of there. But then God spoke to my heart clearly. Unmistakably. "You do an altar call just like you would if there were one hundred fifty people in this room."

So when the music stopped, and Zion was restored to her relationship with God, I stepped forward and gave an invitation to get right with God. "Stand up if you want to receive Jesus," I said in closing.

Then, it happened. General John Rivieta himself stood to his feet. There were tears in his eyes. Four of his other officers did, too. Against all odds, the gospel had reached him. Jesus had reached him.

He pulled Ciro and I aside after that, and he seemed to be a different man. "This is the most incredible thing I've ever seen. We need this. All of our military bases need this. Can you take it to them in the month of March?" March was just two months away. We would have to bring another team. Maybe two teams. But we could figure that out later.

"Yes, we can do that," I said.

But he wanted to make sure I understood. They would transport us, and they would protect us as well as they could, but there was no guarantee that we wouldn't be attacked. This was civil war, after all, and many of the bases were up in the mountains, far from the safety of the kind of compounds we were currently in.

"Yes," I said. "I understand. We can do it."

He asked me one more thing. "Can you bring 32,000 Bibles with you?"

"Sure, we can do that," I said. Of course, I didn't have 32,000 Spanish language Bibles, but what else could I say?

We returned home to Oregon after that and put out the call for new Zion teams. We would take two waves of teams, we decided. They would each be there for two weeks. While our people prayed about who was to go, and how they would raise the money in such a short turnaround, I started thinking about the Bible situation.

How could I find that many Bibles so quickly? And how on earth could I pay for them?

I found a company in Pennsylvania that said they could provide the Bibles at just a dollar apiece. That was perfect. So I got on the phone and called some businessmen I knew to see if we could pull together $32,000.

Somehow, it worked. We got the money, and they shipped the Bibles. We loaded them onto an empty school bus. We took out the seats to make more room to stack the boxes from floor to ceiling. They were so heavy that we had to replace the springs in the bus. Once it was loaded, we sent our drivers ahead to the Mexican border so they could drive straight through to Guatemala where we would meet them.

Unfortunately, there was a hitch. "They won't let us into Mexico!" our drivers reported. "They won't give us the permit to come in!"

They tried three different crossings from Texas to California, but at every location, the border agents turned them away. At last, we gave up and sent the Bibles back to Pennsylvania for a refund, and we all piled onto the plane anyway.

The team was excited about the ministry, and I was, too. By all accounts, this was an unprecedented missions trip. Not only were we going to these military bases, but General Rivieta had also arranged for us to perform Zion on their national TV station. That was the first stop on our itinerary.

But as exciting as all that was, I couldn't shake the feeling of disappointment. I had promised the general I would bring those Bibles, but I couldn't deliver. He would be disappointed. I spent some time talking to God about it all on that flight, and He spoke something surprising to my heart.

"I didn't tell you to get those Bibles."

That was odd. It was true, but it had also seemed like an obvious move for me. I had agreed to provide them, hadn't I? How else could I do that besides actually supplying and transporting them?

"Trust me with Bibles the same way you trust me with the ministry," He seemed to say to my heart. "You didn't figure any of this out, did you? You didn't make any of it happen. I'm the one who did it. I gave you the military in Guatemala. I can give every soldier a Bible. You don't know the mysteries of God."

That, I knew was true. I had learned much following the Holy Spirit, but even after years of service, God remained a mystery. He was still surprising me. So I shrugged and hoped He would surprise me again.

When we landed, we got on a bus and headed for the hotel in Guatemala City. The television performance was happening later in the day, and we needed to go get ourselves cleaned up and ready. Traffic was terrible that day, and we came to a particularly busy roundabout. That was where a young man on a bicycle tried to cross the street. It was a terrible place to cross, and he didn't make it. A small blue Datsun truck plowed into him and ran right over him before coming to a stop. It happened directly in front of us.

I jumped out of my seat and yelled for some of our young, strong students to come out with me. We ran out of the bus and lifted up the back of the truck, fully expecting to find a dead body underneath. But the young man wasn't dead. In fact, he didn't even appear to be injured at all.

He jumped out from under the truck and pulled his broken bike out with him. There was no blood, no scrapes or scratches, nothing! He looked completely unharmed. Before we had a chance to see if he was okay, however, he took off running, holding the mangled mess of metal that used to be his bike.

Our jaws fell open. That pickup, like all Datsuns, was low to the ground. There was no more than twelve inches of clearance. How did he make it through that wreck unscathed? The driver of the Datsun, however, was not unscathed. He was fine, physically, but he was also shaken up. He had almost killed a man! When he got his truck off to the side of the road he got out, and I put my arm around him.

"What's your name?" I asked, and he told me he was Solomon.

"What do you do, Solomon?"

"I'm the Vice President of the Gideons here in Guatemala."

My breath stopped. The Gideons were the largest Bible distributors in the world. No one has ever come close to their achievements. They are the ones who put Bibles in virtually every hotel in the United States, and they have dispersed millions more in countless languages around the world. And this man was the vice president!

"I could kiss you right now!" I exclaimed. And I really could have!

"Why?" He asked.

"Because I need 32,000 Spanish Bibles. Do you have them?"

The man nodded. "I have way more than that," he said.

I got excited. "Can I buy them from you?"

"No," he said. "I'm sorry. We can't sell Bibles. But we can give them away."

I really could have kissed him right then, but I didn't know about the cultural implications of such a move.

"Solomon, please, how can I get my hands on those Bibles?"

"You can't. You have to be a Gideon to deliver them."

"But we're about to go meet with General John Rivieta, and we need to deliver them to the soldiers."

Now, it was Solomon's turn to be aghast. Just like Ronny Coffer, the Gideons had wanted for years to get an opportunity to minister to the army. They had never been allowed. And yet, here we were.

"Come with us," I pleaded. "Please, follow us to the TV station. Then you can join us and deliver the Bibles through our team!"

Later that day, we stood in front of a government-run TV station and performed Zion on live broadcast television. Once again the students performed beautifully, and Ciro and I stood up afterward. I looked into the camera and told the invisible audience about this Jesus, who had redeemed Zion in the play. I asked them to raise their hands if they wanted to receive Jesus, even though I wouldn't be able to see them. The three cameramen did respond, however. They were all soldiers, and they all raised their hands during the filming.

I knew this trip was going to be amazing.

After that, we went back to "the White House" and met with General Riveta again. Right away, he asked me the question: "Did you bring my Bibles?"

"I sure did," I answered.

"Good. I knew I could count on you to do that," he said. I smiled. I don't think I ever told him the whole story of how it all happened. But then, I'm not sure I could have explained it if I tried? Could I possibly explain what had just happened in the street that day? Did I have any clue how that young biker had survived the crash, or how he had run away without a scratch? Could I make sense of how we ended up directly behind the only man in Guatemala who could deliver 32,000 Bibles into our hands?

No. None of it made any sense. I've even wondered about the biker himself. Did God wrap him in divine bubble wrap under that truck? Was he an angel? The scriptures say that sometimes we entertain angels unawares, doesn't it? Hebrews 13:2. Who knows? I don't claim to understand the mysteries of God.

However it all happened, General Riveta was pleased, and he sent us on our way. There were thirty-two military bases. They would fly us from base to base in military planes or transport us on their buses. We would often stay in the barracks, and eat with the men. We would be under the protection of the military with one job, to spread the gospel of Jesus Christ to more than thirty thousand soldiers.

It didn't take long, however, for our new friend Solomon to realize how impossible it would be for him to operate as a traditional Gideon. After we visited the first base, did the drama, and saw the hundreds of hands go up, we had to hand out more than six hundred bibles. It was way too many for him. He became overwhelmed, and we still had two more bases to go to that very day!

"Solomon, our team can help you. Let us help you."

But he shook his head. "I can't. In order to pass out Gideon Bibles, you have to be a Gideon."

I smiled. "Then Solomon, why don't you deputize us? Make us Gideons for the month of March?"

He thought on that for a second. I'm sure there were rules against this kind of thing, but the merit of the idea outweighed the potential bureaucratic discrepancies. Our team stood in a line, raised our right hands, and swore to faithfully disperse Bibles to the soldiers of Nicaragua through the month of March. It was official. Sort of. We were Gideons.

For the next four weeks, our two waves of Zion teams piled on tail dragger planes and hopped from army base to army base. These were military planes, but they transported lots of civilians. Villagers often loaded up with us, carrying pigs and chickens and other non-traditional luggage.

The planes were small, and they didn't have the usual seats. We sat on the floor along the walls and tried not to focus on the rickety construction of the plane. But that was hard to do when we could see through the cracks around the door. It was a good thing we were flying low or else we would have lost all the cabin pressure.

The whole month was an incredible adventure: planes, buses, vans, and crates of endless Bibles. There was always muggy heat in the lowlands and a chill in the mountains. And there were soldiers…so many soldiers. Everywhere we went, we did Zion, and everywhere we did Zion, hundreds of men responded to the Gospel. We had a tight schedule to keep so we could never stay for long. But how can you say no when a dozen soldiers come up after a performance asking for prayer? How do you say no when the fields are so white unto harvest? (John 4:35)

When all was said and done, we had successfully ministered in all thirty-two military bases in Guatemala. By our count, we gave away over thirty thousand Bibles, and more than twenty-three thousand soldiers had said yes to Jesus Christ. It was one of the most electrifying experiences I have ever had.

Soldiers receiving Bibles from Solomon, head of the Gideons in Guatemala

At the end of that whirlwind tour, General Riveta said he wanted to throw a banquet in our honor as a way of saying thank you. The generals were thrilled at what they saw from our team, and John Riveta was ecstatic. For him, it wasn't just about personal salvation. It was about hope for Guatemala. He believed that if a third world nation like his own was ever to join the developing world, it needed Christianity. In his view, we had helped deliver the Christian faith to a country that desperately needed it.

I was honored that they wanted to throw a banquet, and I asked if we could invite the Gideons since they had helped to make it happen. He gladly agreed.

So I went back to our hotel in Guatemala City and rested, waiting for the phone call that would give us more information on the banquet itself. I was poolside when the call came to the front desk.

"Mr. Bowers," the secretary said when I picked up, "General Rivieta regrets to inform you that the banquet is canceled. Thank you for all you've done. Goodbye." At that, she hung up. I was not terribly surprised. John Rivieta was a busy man, after all. So I began searching for Solomon's phone number to let him know there would be no banquet.

In just a few minutes, however, another call came.

"Mr. Bowers. The banquet will take place this evening 4:30 this afternoon. Please be ready." And she hung up again. I was baffled!

They transported us down to the restaurant that afternoon. The kitchen was busy, but the tables were empty. Deserted. It was obvious they had cleared out the place for this event.

"Mr. Bowers, thank you so much for coming," our host said.

"What's going on? Why the two phone calls?" I asked him.

The man smiled. "These are important officers we're dealing with, Mr. Bowers. We had to cancel the banquet with the first call because people might be listening in. The second phone call was more secure."

Then, he pointed across the empty restaurant to a man in a long jacket.

"See that cook over there? He's not a cook. He's actually one of us." The man caught our eye, pulled back his jacket, and revealed a sawed-off shotgun.

I shook my head. What was going on here?

"Follow me," the man said, and we went up on the roof.

"Look there, and there, and there," he said, pointing to the armed guards on every corner. They were surrounding the restaurant.

Then he pointed to the yellow taxicabs. I couldn't miss them. They were everywhere. So many, in fact, that the streets were essentially clogged. "Those drivers are all soldiers." They had the place utterly surrounded and insulated from attack.

Soon, the other guests began arriving. And they weren't strangers, either. We knew them at once. They were generals from the different bases we had visited. But they weren't alone. They had their wives with them.

They came in car after car, one high-ranking official after another. They greeted us with the familiar excitement that only exists between old friends. We embraced them and shared our recent memories.

Soon, the restaurant was full. Not every general was present, but most of them were there, representing the thirty-two bases we had ministered at. There were around sixty military personnel, forty Gideons, and twenty-five Oregonians, mostly teenagers. And everywhere you looked, there was joy in this unlikely coalition. It was clear to all of us that God had done a truly great work.

After a few minutes, the final two guests arrived: who else but General John Rivieta and his wife?

We embraced, and I laughed. "This has been the most confusing day of my life! First, the banquet is canceled and then it's on. Then you're not coming, and now you're here!"

The general smiled. "Jon, Look around you," he said. "See all these generals? What do you think would happen if the wrong people found out we were all together in one room?" It was a grave moment in one way, but an incredible honor, too. This was the effect our trip had had. It was so great that these men took a calculated strategic risk in order to acknowledge the profound impact of the gospel on their nation.

I shared the gospel once more that evening, and three more invited Jesus into their lives. All three were wives of the generals.

We went back to Guatemala more times after that. Once, we visited ten bases and baptized innumerable men in the ocean and in swimming pools. Another time, we brought thousands and thousands of dollars worth of Christmas presents for the children of the poor soldiers we ministered to. Each time we went, it seemed the officials afforded us a little more freedom. We weren't allowed to preach the first time; but by the end, we could do pretty much whatever we wanted to do, and go wherever we wanted to go. The impact was incredible.

The generals weren't the only ones who took note of that great adventure. One of our hotel hosts was an American whose father ran a large and influential Christian magazine in the United States. He asked us to perform Zion for the hotel staff. We did, and we told him the entire story of all God had done. The man was so impressed that he called his father and told him the story.

When we returned to Oregon, his father called me and told me he wanted the story. He wanted to put me on the cover of his magazine. He wanted to publish the entire account. This was a big deal, and Christians around the world would want to hear the story, he said. He wanted to get me speaking at conferences around the globe. He wanted to make me a household name in the Christian world.

I listened to his offer, and I liked it. I liked it a lot. I told him to go ahead and send his photographer and editor to Oregon. We would do the story.

But something happened when I hung up the phone. My secretary, Sharron Stevens, came around the corner with a little tear in her eye. She had heard me preach about the importance of keeping our heads down. If we work together and stop caring who gets the credit, I would say, there is no limit to what God can do through us. But now I was going back on that. I was accepting all the credit.

In truth, I deserved none of it.

Sure, I had been obedient and bold, but this move of God hadn't come about through me. It had come through one divine encounter after another: a struggling addict with a missionary zeal, a burned-out plane engine and an emergency landing. A CIA operative who happened to be friends with Ronny Coffer, a powerful general with a tender heart to the gospel, a Bible man and an indestructible bicyclist, and thousands of hungry souls being met by a living Holy Spirit. None of it was my doing. I don't know the mysteries of God, after all!

So I canceled the interview. I decided that if I wanted God to keep doing great things, I had no business parading out the old ones. He had just given us a nation. And soon enough, if we kept our heads down, He would give us another one.

Chapter 13: The Alliance

When you're riding a wave like we were riding in Guatemala, there is nothing more exhilarating. It seemed every risk we took paid off. Every act of boldness was rewarded. Everywhere we looked, people were breaking down and giving their lives to Jesus. Once in the book of Acts, Luke recorded that "The word of the Lord grew mightily and prevailed." (Acts 19:20) That's how it felt in Guatemala. God was prevailing. He was winning. And let me tell you something…it was FUN.

Most people think ministry is supposed to be serious business, and I suppose they're half-right. It requires hard work, financial planning, dedication, and many hours of prayer, after all. But when God shows up and starts moving, you can't help but loosen your tie a little and enjoy the ride.

Even in the less glamorous times when we're not sharing planes with villagers and sharing the gospel with heads of state, the work of the Lord is meant to be shared, savored, and celebrated. So, when I was at the office with my staff at Christ's Center I made sure we took time to play. We had impromptu trips to the donut shop, day trips to the beach, and inner tube trips down the river. We had picnics, movies and loads of laughter. Are those productive times? Not in the traditional sense, no. But when you play together, you start to build stronger relationships, which then become the conduit through which the Spirit of God does great things.

Long before the Guatemala expedition, I had developed all kinds of friendships with other missionaries and ministry leaders. Many of them doing the hard work of soul harvest all over the world. None of them needed another meeting. What they needed was fellowship. What they needed was fun, just like I needed it.

So, we would gather a couple times every year to have intentional fun. Sometimes it was for a weekend in the mountains of Colorado. Sometimes it was a few days on the Oregon coast. And sometimes it was a night in one another's living room. The location didn't matter. Wherever we were, we would hang out, laugh a lot, have adventures, and share life. We talked about ministry too, of course, but that was never the focus. I would say to them over and over, "don't take ministry so seriously that you get heartburn."

That message—that mantra—began to take hold over time. We all realized how much we needed these little respites from the pressures of leading. They fed our souls. Negiel Bigpond was introduced to the Alliance. A Native American chief of the Uchee tribe, and a highly respected, influential Christian leader among many tribes. So Negiel joined us, as did other pastors from all across the United States.

Thus our little group began to grow not only in numbers, but in variety, background and culture.

It was only when we struck up that friendship with our Harlem friends at Bethel Gospel Assembly, that "The Alliance" really took off. It went from being just a small group of ministers playing together to a large, diverse group of Jesus-lovers playing together.

I'll never forget the first time we all gathered in Junction City. Bishop Williams put his whole staff on a plane, and then some. More than eighty people came from their church and many more from other churches around the country. Christ's Center families opened up their homes to host them, and for a few days, we spent time playing and praying together.

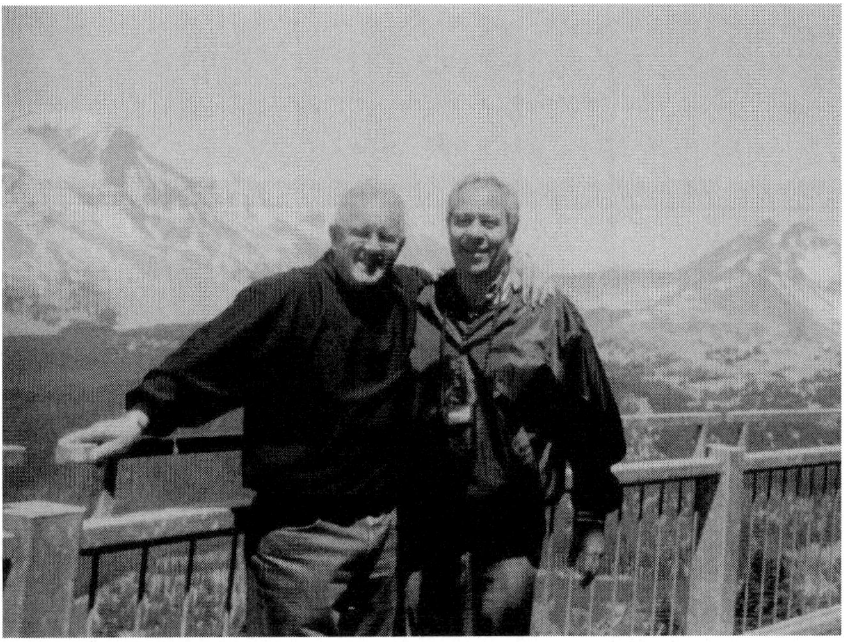

Jon and Alejandro on a vacation in the Oregon cascades. This was the first snow Alijhandro ever experienced.

The highlight of that week was our trip rafting down the Mackenzie River. Oregon is blessed to have such a wide variety of exotic terrain, and we were eager to show it off to our friends on inflatable rafts. Many of our Harlem guests, however, had never seen river rapids before, let alone ridden on them. It was an adventure they would not soon forget. The day trip started out with the nervous tightening of life jackets, but it ended with an epic super-soaker right there in the river.

We laughed for hours that week, and we worshipped for hours, too. Corporate worship became another hallmark of those gatherings, and they were never dull. Bethel's praise team came, and when their gospel choir started singing, the hair on your arms would stand up. It was unforgettable. Our Christ's Center worship leaders led the music right alongside Harlem's, and all our people stood side by side, glorifying God together with one voice. It was the first of many wild and beautiful worship experiences we would have together.

That first large gathering went so well that we decided we needed to keep right on doing it. We would gather twice a year in our various locations, we decided, and we would open our doors to whoever wanted to join.

Over the next few years, this budding alliance expanded and Negiel Bigpond became a major player in it. In our assemblies, he would sometimes wear the regalia of the Native American chief that he was, complete with the headdress and feathers.

Then, the cowboys came. If you've never seen a cowboy church in action, you're missing out. They wear hats and vests—the whole cowboy getup—and they sing old-school country gospel music. It's an experience unlike any other. And Tom Crabb—the man I had once told not to let his desire to "raise hell" keep him out of heaven—had become the pastor of his own cowboy church right in Junction City, Oregon. Bishop Williams was always tickled about the fact that we not only had black folk and white folk at our gatherings, we even had "cowboys and Indians" too, all worshipping together as brothers.

Those days of praise and play knit our hearts together in powerful ways. Even though we as leaders didn't see each other all that often, we became very close. Whenever a crisis arose, we came together. We jumped on planes when family members fell ill. We also joined in times of celebrations at weddings and graduations. Our hearts grew closer to one another, and closer to God as well

Pastor Gordon Williams of Harlem New York, Jon Bowers and Chief Negiel Bigpond of Oklahoma attendees at Dr. Jay Swallow's grave side service in Oklahoma.

The group didn't have a name. At first, we called our gatherings "Pastor's Conference," even though we were trying very hard not to make our gatherings conferences. But soon, we started referring to the group as "the Alliance."

The Alliance was an entirely relational entity. There were no financial ties, no doctrinal statement, no office to report to. It was simply a group of friends who wanted to glorify God and enjoy Him together. People would ask us, "How do I join the Alliance?" We would say, "You want to join? You're in!" Of course, it wasn't for everyone. Our lack of form was always a problem for those who craved tight schedules and heady Bible studies. Those ones didn't usually last long, but we were okay with that. This group wasn't about structure. It was all about relationship.

One of the greatest shared passions among the Alliance members was international missions. We had Youth With A Mission leaders among us for one thing, but it went way beyond that. Bethel Gospel Assembly had their own rich history of international ministry, and they were doing wonderful things around the globe. And of course, Christ's Center was experiencing that glorious favor among the army of Guatemala.

So, it's no surprise that as we shared those testimonies, we began sharing plane rides, too. Together, the Alliance ministered in India and Venezuela; Mexico and Grenada; Nicaragua and Russia. We went all over the place! And while we went, we often bumped into new people who wanted to join us—brothers and sisters working overseas for the Lord who needed relief from the "heartburn." Soon, our coalition included Pastor Paul from Russia, and Pastor Tony from India, and two couples from Cuba.

Christ's Center remained right at the center of all the action over these years. The mid 90's came and went, and we were creeping toward the turn of the century. I invited a man named Dave Kaufman to be my associate pastor. He began to carry many of the day-to-day operations at Christ's Center while I focused more and more on outreach with our Alliance friends. I loved spurring our people on to go to the nations. I used to tell the congregation, "Get your passports ready," and they did, because they didn't want to miss out, either.

At one Alliance conference in the late '90s, a man named Jay Swallow joined us. Jay was Negiel Bigpond's mentor. He was a chief in the Cheyenne tribe and was considered a chief over many Native American chiefs. Seriously. When a tribe had serious issues to navigate or disputes so settle, they brought Jay in to help bring a resolution. And just like Negiel, Jay was a powerful Christian man, a well of fervent prayer and deep wisdom. It was truly an amazing thing that God had these two saints in such influential positions.

We had already become friends with Jay through Negiel, and over the years, we had tried like crazy to get Jay to join the Alliance. But he had thus far shown no interest in it whatsoever. Finally, that year, we prevailed upon him to at least come and see what all the fuss was about.

Christ's Center was hosting the conference that year, and I was in charge of the evening's gathering. We would have worship, and we also had a speaker scheduled, but as the meeting began, I felt like God was stirring me to change our evening plans. I felt like Michael O'Barr, our friend with Down's syndrome, ought to bring the word that night.

So I asked Michael, and he agreed. He wasn't particularly thrilled about it—he got nervous in front of crowds—but he agreed.

There were three hundred people in our auditorium that night, at least. Michael might have been nervous at first, but when he got going, he spoke in the same way he always did.

"I'm not a speaker, but let me tell you, I'm happy." He went on to give the same short talk I'd watched him give a dozen times before. He spoke boldly about the overwhelming joy of the Lord in his own life, and how it was available to them as well. It was a five-minute sermon, just like always.

And just like always, there were tears throughout the audience. He had moved them. They had felt their own need for more of the joy of the Lord. He stretched out his hands and prayed for the entire crowd. It was vintage Michael.

The next morning, our guest Jay Swallow asked me to go to coffee with him. When we sat down to talk, he became emotional, which was a wonder in itself. Jay never showed emotion in public. Ever. But this time, he began to weep as he recounted what had happened the night before.

"I knew you had taken Michael in like a son," he said. "And I knew you brought him with you places like you would a sidekick, but when you had him come up and speak, it broke me to my core." He took a breath. "You see, my daughter is mentally handicapped. And because of that, nobody would have ever put her onstage at a major gathering. Because you just did that with Michael, and because you have honored him like that, I'm all in."

I was overjoyed. Jay and I became even closer friends after that, and he became a pillar in the Alliance.

We went on growing like that for years. God kept adding to our numbers, and He kept sending us into new places.

Another year, Bishop Williams gave the evening message. We were gathered in the barn of the Eugene cattle auction. That was where Cowboy Church met every week. Bishop Williams was fascinated by the Cowboy Church culture, and I think the cowboys were fascinated with him. When he came with several dozen others from Harlem, they were greeted not only with a strong manure smell they had never experienced before, but with smoldering summer heat. It was hot and stinky in that barn.

Nevertheless, he preached with fire, and he had the entire crowd—cowboys, Indians, white folk, black folk and Latinos, the list goes on and on—eating out of his hand. Nobody preached like my friend Ezra.

"You know what I think?" he said that night. "I think we oughta hold the conference in Harlem next year."

And everyone agreed. The next year, we gathered in Harlem.

The year was 2003, and I carry many memories from that conference. I remember meeting one evening in Bethel's auditorium. It was packed out with over a thousand people. I remember how Negiel Bigpond became a star by wearing the feathered headdress of his Uchee tribe. Everyone wanted to meet him. I remember taking a huge group of people to Yankee Stadium to take in a baseball game. I remember people enjoying one another at Broadway shows and various New York attractions. And I remember almost stopping traffic with our strange looking kingdom contingent.

But more than anything, I remember the outrageous thing God spoke to us about Cuba. The 2003 conference was the first time our Cuban pastor friends had ever been able to join us. These were two powerful couples: Eliseo and Bobbi Acosta were Assemblies of God pastors in Havana, overseeing dozens of other churches in that denomination. Alejandro and Alida Nita pastored one of the most vibrant, dynamic churches I have ever had the pleasure of experiencing in any nation. Alejandro was a magnetic speaker, too, and so influential, people called him "the Billy Graham of Cuba."

Of course, the Cuban government was not very friendly to Christian churches at the time. As a communist power, they have never smiled upon the faith community. Ever since Fidel Castro's rise to power in the 1950s, thousands of Christians have been imprisoned or killed for their faith. Our friends had experienced first hand the brutal sting of religious persecution in their nation. The government let their churches stay in operation so long as they didn't rock the boat too much, but they were heavily monitored. Pastors had to live with constant intimidation, knowing that at any moment, their doors could be closed, and their freedom could be taken away forever.

Alejandro, Michael O'barr, and Eliseo

So, it was a real treat for these couples to join us in New York City. They loved being with us almost as much as we loved being with them.

One evening of that week, the Alliance pastors assembled to pray about the location of the next year's gathering. The hotel had double-booked their conference room that evening, so they cleared out the bar and let us meet there. It was a strange, almost ironic twist.

There had already been a lot of chatter about holding the next conference in the city of Lucknow, India, since one of our own, Pastor Tony, ministered there. It was our tradition, however, to pray about it together. Nobody made unilateral decisions in the Alliance.

So that night, I stood up in front of the group and announced our topic of prayer, and we all fell silent, listening for the voice of the Lord. In that silence, the name of a city rose in my heart. It came with such force, I knew it was God—Havana, Cuba.

But of course, it made no sense. It was absurd. Even more absurd than bidding $100,000 on a church property, or bringing a mime team to Harlem. It might have even more absurd than sharing the gospel with thirty thousand Guatemalan soldiers. Cuba was a closed nation, after all, with no freedom of assembly. They were hostile to our country and to our faith. And if that weren't enough, the Cuban church, for all their rugged and sincere faith, was terribly skittish about getting together. They had seen too much persecution to ever gather so publicly. They knew what would happen if they did: the government would see them as a growing threat, and they would put an end to it.

All of these truths flashed through my mind in the silence of that bar room, but I couldn't escape the whispers of God to my heart.

"It's Havana. Say it in faith. Speak it by my Spirit."

So I stood up again. "Guys, I can't explain it, but I'm hearing Cuba."

There was no fanfare at that pronouncement. In fact, nobody spoke at all. It was a moment almost awkward as it was shocking. The only sound was the laughter that broke out a moment later.

"I'm serious, guys," I told them. "Mark my words, this time next year, we will be having our conference in Havana, Cuba."

The Cubans who were with us said nothing at first, but I could tell they weren't warm to the idea, and nobody else knew what to think. So we decided to shelve the matter that night and decide on the following evening.

The next day, I had a talk with my friend Alejandro. For some people, the idea of gathering in Cuba sounded like exotic, delicious fun, but this man shared no glee in my vision. For him, this was personal. He knew the lay of the land. He knew what was at stake. This one wasn't about fun. This was serious business.

I'll never forget the words he said to me over that table, "Pastor, I would believe God could sooner part the waters from Havana to Miami than have a conference in Cuba."

He walked away after that, but God was working on him, I could tell. He came back to me an hour later and asked me if I was serious, if I really thought God was leading us to meet in Havana.

"Yes, I do." I said.

He took a breath and said some of bravest words I have ever heard, "Then let the waters part."

That same night, the Alliance pastors agreed, and the matter was settled. We were going to Cuba.

Chapter 14: Cuba

"It's never been done before." That's what people kept telling me. A gathering of Protestant leaders in a communist country had never happened under the reign of Fidel Castro. And because it hadn't been done, people were afraid to consider the possibility that it could happen. There were just so many risks.

I could hardly blame them for that. After all, wasn't I the one that had avoided the world map in the hallway for all those years? No, these saints were simply looking at the situation with human eyes. In the material world, they were right to doubt our plans. This had never been done before. The government of Cuba was hostile to the faith.

But I was all in now. I was trying to invest every talent I had. So what did it matter that this particular thing had never been done before? What did that have to do with anything? Wasn't God in the business of doing new things?

For me, it was as simple as this: God had spoken, and I wanted to obey. Indeed, I wanted to obey whenever He spoke, whatever the situation. In this instance, I felt as if I was standing on a diving board but couldn't see the water. And yet I knew if God said, "jump" the water would fill. When God tells us to take risks, He meets us there. He makes things happen. He gives us an experience we won't soon forget.

Going to Cuba is always a fascinating experience. The first thing you notice is the natural beauty. It's a land of hot, sandy beaches and picturesque palms standing guard over the mighty Caribbean. The next thing you notice is the eclectic mix of new and old, facade and reality, the pretty picture and the heartbreaking truth. One building is freshly adorned with ornate colorful spires in the European fashion, the next one is suffering the final stages of dilapidation and decay.

The roads themselves are wonders. You'll see a classic Chevy in perfect show-car condition driving alongside a rusty roadster, held together by ingenuity and duct tape. Cuba's closed markets have forced the people to keep the old stuff running as long as they possibly can because that is all they were going to get. Since there are almost no new cars, they do whatever they can to keep their old ones running. Their mechanics are real miracle workers.

The exotic landscape and the warm, colorful culture make Cuba a popular destination spot, especially for European vacationers. When we visited, we stayed at the popular Melia Cohiba Hotel, which sits right on the ocean. It's a beautiful spot, complete with all the amenities first-world westerners crave: air conditioning, fine restaurants, a luxurious pool, and a sprawling conference room. The whole experience is meant to convince you that Communism has been a great success for Cuba, but it is simply an elaborate con. All you have to do is ask one of the locals about places like the Melia Cohiba, and they'll tell you the truth, those are for the tourists only. Actual Cubans aren't even allowed to step foot inside.

The average Cuban worker makes roughly eight dollars per month and lacks many of the basic freedoms we in America take for granted. Freedom of Assembly, for instance, is not a cherished right. If you want to gather in Cuba, you have to either do it in secret, or you have to get permission. And even if you ask permission, you have to be careful. If you ask for something too audacious, the asking itself can land you in jail.

As we began to plan our own assembly of believers in

Havana, we knew we would have to work with the government and not against it. This would not be a quiet, underground meeting in the shadows. No. Many churches had already been doing that for sixty years. We had something different in mind, a colorful, loud, harmonious gaggle of saints all praising God in the open and without fear. We wanted to make a statement that could not possibly be misconstrued—Jesus is Lord. Even here. We had to be upfront about such intentions. We had to ask permission.

That was a daunting prospect for my friend Alejandro. The first thing he told me was that he expected to be arrested for making such a proposal.

Nevertheless, I felt immense peace about my friend's well being. If God was directing us—and I was certain that He was—then He would surely take care of this precious man and his family. "No one will go to jail." Those were the words I heard in my spirit.

There were practical reasons for my confidence, too. The Alliance had something I knew might appeal to the Cuban government, we had diversity. We had cowboys with guitars and ten-gallon hats and Native Americans with drums and feathers. We had real Indians—from India, I mean—Mexicans, white Americans, and an African American gospel choir. We knew how to put all of those colors and cultures together to make something beautiful. Cuba was always looking for good international photo ops, and our worship services would fit the bill. This event, I was sure, would provide them with a low-risk way to get some good public relations points.

So, while we began to plan back in the states, Pastor Alejandro led the charge in Cuba. He enlisted the help of another man—Pastor Hector Hunter, the head of the Assemblies of God in Cuba. Since they were the largest Protestant denomination in the country, Hector had the ear of every one of the thirty-nine denominational heads in the nation.

These two men, along with our friend Pastor Eliseo, were the three most influential pastors in the nation. The government had reason to consider their proposal. Still, though, not everyone was convinced any of it would matter. The government comprised only part of the problem. There was also the church itself to contend with.

Cuban pastors were accustomed to keeping their heads down and going about their work as quietly as possible so as not to make a stir. Joining an event like this could easily turn them targets for government reprisals. Hector knew this better than anyone. He had lived through some dark, dark days in Cuba. He had seen first hand both the brutality of the state and the resulting fears of the people.

"It's impossible, Jon," Hector told me. "It will never happen in my lifetime."

My stubbornness rose up within me when he said that, and I countered. "You will see it in your lifetime. This time next year you'll see it happen in this city. All thirty-nine leaders will come."

And so we went to work. The denominational leaders had never brought themselves together in a small setting before, let alone in a big one with hundreds of flag-waving, Jesus following internationals. So they sent invitations to all thirty-nine of those leaders. They called them to gather on the rooftop of Alejandro's church in Havana on an appointed night. There, God willing, when they came to that small setting, they would meet me, and I would tell them all about this big meeting God was arranging. It would be a hard sell, but I knew it was possible if they would only come out of the shadows.

When the appointed night arrived, my three friends were nervous that nobody would show up. And in the end, they were right. Not a single pastor came. That was a real blow, a setback for us all. These leaders had reasons to be fearful. They had spent years worrying about government informants, police raids, and arbitrary arrests. They were dealing with a Communist dictatorship that had oppressed them their entire lives. They never knew who they could trust, and they weren't about to do the bidding of this strange Oregonian pastor who may or may not be an informant himself!

Nevertheless, we remained undaunted. God had spoken. I was sure of it. So while the pastoral angle stalled out, we kept working on the government. Alejandro made the official request, and Ciro and I began taking trips down to Havana to meet with the authorities.

When he arranged a meeting with the officials, it was at Fidel Castro's compound. Alejandro warned us before we went in that our car would be bugged on the drive home. The secret police would probably sneak in and hide it somewhere, so whatever happened inside, we needed to keep our conversation pleasant and positive. This was Cuba. There was no freedom of assembly, and there was no privacy, either.

A guard met us at the waiting room and took us up an elevator to the third floor. He led us to a small interrogation room. It was plain and windowless, and a short, vague contraption hung from the ceiling—a camera and a microphone. They had tried to disguise it a little, but it was impossible to miss.

The guard left us there, and in a few minutes, our man came in to meet us. I'll call him Matthew, and he was fit to be tied.

"You think we would ever let you do something like this in Cuba? Fidel Castro will never sanction this meeting. Just who do you Americans think you are, anyway?" Then, the man launched into the most impressive anti-American diatribe I'd ever heard. He told us all the ways our country was awful, and all the reasons we ought to be ashamed. He even told me what I could tell George W. Bush the next time I saw him. For fifteen minutes he dressed us down like an army drill sergeant. It could not have gone any worse.

But then, abruptly, Matthew stopped.

"Would you guys like some cookies? Maybe a cup of coffee?"

We looked at one another, stunned.
"Sure." we said.

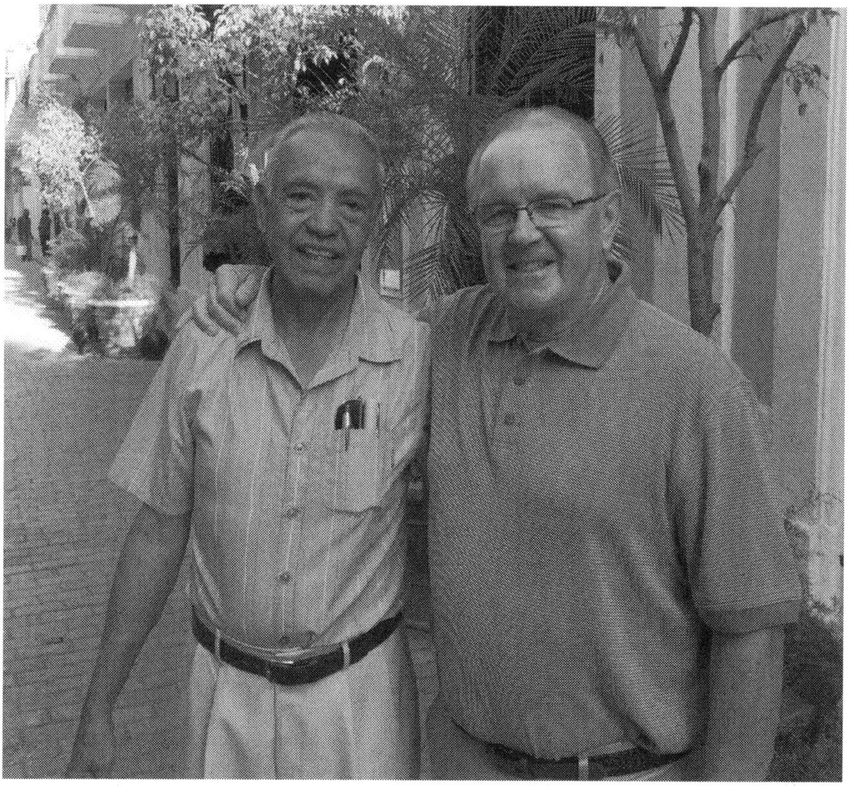

Jon with Ciro Guiterrez, his interpreter for thirty years, on one of many trips to Cuba

He rang a little bell, and the door swung open on command, letting in a lady pushing a cart with a silver tray of refreshments. And just like that, everything changed. The man became cordial. Friendly, even.

"So, when do you think you'd like to do this conference?" He asked.

We told him and gave him a vague outline of our plan. He

listened politely to our answers.

"Well, it's not going to happen," he said when we were finished, but without the heat of his earlier performance.

On the drive home, we talked about how kind everyone at the compound was, and what a pleasant experience it had been. When we got out, we found the surveillance bug in the car and promptly destroyed it.

Matthew, we decided, had simply been playing to the cameras. He needed it on record, he had dutifully lambasted us like a good official ought. He had proven his worth as a guardian of Cuban norms. But his heart had never really been in it. In fact, we could tell that Matthew had already started taking a liking to Ciro, which was no surprise. Everyone takes a liking to Ciro. He's one of the friendliest, most interesting men I've ever known.

So even though the door had been effectively slammed in our faces, we remained undeterred. I went home to Oregon but flew back again with Ciro in a matter of weeks. We had another meeting at the compound. And once again, a guard took us up the elevator to the third floor, and into the interrogation room.

In came Matthew, his face twisted with rage against us and our nation. He ranted again about America, and then, after fifteen minutes, rang the bell and ushered in the silver tray of snacks. It was total dèjá vu.

"It really isn't going to happen," he assured us, even while he and Ciro laughed and talked in Spanish.

Again I flew home empty-handed. But I was sure God had spoken!

After that, there were more identical meetings, and I began bringing other members of the alliance with me. I wanted to let the officials see these men in the flesh, men like Negiel Bigpond, and Gordon Williams. And no matter who I brought in, we got the same fifteen-minute grilling, then the bell and the silver snack cart.

But persistence paid off, eventually. It was on our ninth or tenth trip to Havana that Matthew asked, "Where do you want to do the conference?"

I was ready for that question. I already had the arrangements in place. "At the Melia Cohiba Hotel. That's where we stay when we come here."

"Well," he said, "if you can get Havana Tours to sign off on it, then you can have your conference."

We were elated. Ciro and I had already become well acquainted with the hotel staff by then. Most of them were eating out of Ciro's hand! We knew they would welcome the business of hundreds of international travelers.

Havana Tours, the tourist agency, is an entirely government-run operation. We had to convince them not only about the hotel arrangements but about buses and transportation. Most importantly, if we were going to have the conference in the Melia Cohiba, we had to convince them to allow the Cuban people themselves to join us.

It was a tough sell, but after just two meetings, Havana Tours signed off on the whole thing. God be praised, we had permission to have our conference!

I went back and told my three pastor friends the news, and their faith was bolstered. "Jon, I'm going to go personally invite all thirty-nine denominational leaders to come to my rooftop," Alejandro told me. "I'm going to convince them that you are not a government informant. We will make this happen."

And bless him, he did just that. He drove all around the country to meet with every single one of those men who had stood him up the first time. "This is God," he said. "And I promise you, it's safe. Come and join us."

Then, the appointed night came. It was May of 2004. Once again, we waited at Alejandro's church. His wife Alida—every bit the firebrand of a leader her husband was—waited there with us. Eliseo was there, too, with his wife Bobbi. They are one of the warmest, most Christ-like couples I've ever known. And of course, Hector, adorned in his quiet wisdom and unshakeable faith. The moment was not lost on me. I was standing beside the leaders of a nation's church at a crucial point in their history. It was a high honor.

"Lord, please just let them all show up this time!"

God answered our prayers that night. One pastor came, then another, then another. They came in like men being followed. They looked over their shoulders and spoke in hushed tones. The suspicion was as thick as the Caribbean humidity.

They continued to trickle in, and before we knew it, they had all arrived. All thirty-nine leaders of Cuba's protestant churches, gathered in one place. God be praised! It was the first time since the Cuban revolution that the church had ever dared gather together like that. Just their presence was a historic victory.

You could see it on their faces, though. They were scared. And part of it had to do with one particular pastor they hadn't counted on.

"Jon, we have a problem," one of them told me. Then he pointed to a man they had not expected to come. "That man. He works with the government. He is a known informant. What should we do?"

"We don't have to worry about him," I said.

Alejandro's church had prepared a rooftop banquet for us that evening. We shared a prayer, shared a meal, and then we got down to business. Alejandro introduced me as the man who was making this whole thing happen.

I thanked them all for coming and told them how much I admired them for their faith. I explained to them all about the Alliance, about how God had moved among us, and how He had spoken clearly about our next conference. We wanted these men, assembled on this rooftop, to be a part of it. We wanted to use our conference to do something unprecedented for Cuba, to bring the church together as one.

I told them I was not a government informant but, I had been clear with the government about my intentions since the beginning. They knew exactly what we wanted to do, and were allowing it. We would hold the conference at the Melia Cohiba, and everyone, including the Cubans, would be let in. They would be equals at the table, and nobody—not even a secret informant on the inside—could do anything about it, because we had permission.

When I was finished, Alejandro took the microphone and personally greeted every man in attendance. He thanked them for coming, and honored their service to God's kingdom. Then, he asked them one question, "Are you in?"

One by one, they spoke into the microphone. All thirty-nine of them gave their answer—yes.

By the time the evening ended, there were no more nervous glances into the shadows. The laughter was no longer restrained, the conversation no longer muted. Everyone talked and laughed and embraced one another, unafraid and eager.

I stood back and watched history unfold. God was doing it. He was parting the waters and raising up his church.

The Alliance was exuberant, of course. The next two months were a blur of fundraising and phone calls and flight itineraries and "How many people are you bringing again?" We were communicating constantly, trying to make sense of what was about to happen.

When July rolled around, two hundred and ten foreigners descended on Havana. We came from places like Aruba, Oklahoma, New Jersey, Arizona, and Russia, but the biggest contingents came from Harlem and Oregon.

The air conditioning was out when we arrived, and the heat was sweltering, but that couldn't dampen our spirits. We began getting our people into their proper hotel rooms and organizing all the registration information. We had to make special name-tags for everyone at the event, especially the Cubans, so they would be allowed in. The hotel still required them to eat their meals off the premises instead of in the restaurants, so we prepared special meals that they could eat outside.

We had to break the meetings up into fifteen-minute increments, in accordance with the rules of the government officials that were present. If they were trying to hide their identities, they were doing a poor job of it. They all sat on the second row of the auditorium wearing conspicuous white shirts, and they were waiting—hoping, I think—for a mistake. They didn't look happy about being there. One misstep and we knew they could put a stop to the conference and throw us out.

We prayed for God's favor, and right away, we knew He was giving it to us. It happened when I saw Ciro arguing with the man in charge. He was a very high-ranking official who reported to Castro himself. Just minutes before we were set to open the conference, this official had suddenly (and arbitrarily) decided that there were simply too many people in the auditorium. He wanted to put a smaller cap on the crowd, which would have forced many people to leave. I could tell he was getting under the skin of some of the other Alliance leaders. It was a tense moment.

Instead of engaging the conflict directly, I took a different tact.

"I want you all to meet someone," I told the packed crowd inside the auditorium. Then, I called the man onstage and told them all how this man had helped us every step of the way, and how grateful we were for his assistance in making the conference happen. At that, the crowd erupted into an appreciative standing ovation.

Red and Loveta Crabb next to Alida and Pastor Alejandro of Cuba

The official's face turned red. Whether he was embarrassed or touched or both, I'll never know, but he left us alone after that. We were thankful. We had important kingdom work to do.

So one by one, we went about our work. The International Alliance leaders fired up the crowd with stories of what God was doing around the world. Christ's Center brought a Zion team and performed onstage. Harlem, with their magnificent choir and passion, brought the soul. The Oregon Cowboys played, too. Pastor Tom Crabb led on the guitar with the magnificent Dale

Keasy on the fiddle, and together, with these many expressions of the same kingdom, we brought the house down.

"Let's take communion together," I said to the leaders during a break.

Nobody liked the idea at first. It was risky. It was the kind of symbolism that the government contingent might find ominous. The last thing authoritarians want to do is allow those they control to band together. That's why they seek to keep people separated. They don't want them to unify. And what greater symbol of unification is there than the Lord's supper?

"This could end it, Jon," they told me. And I knew they were right. It could end it.

But after we talked and prayed together, we decided to double down on unity. Not only would we take communion together, but we would also have a foot washing ceremony. The same kind Bishop Ezra Williams and I had shared more than ten years earlier.

That evening, we took the bread and wine, taking no heed of denominational decorum. The traditions didn't matter. What mattered was that we were brothers and sisters in Jesus.

Then, I washed Bishop Carlton Brown's feet, and he washed mine, and just like that, the floodgates opened. Pastors and leaders all over the room followed our example, which was really Jesus' example, of intimate, sacrificial service. This was nowhere more poignant than among the Cuban pastors—over seventy of whom were present. They had never before shared communion with people outside their immediate denomination. The walls were too high—walls of fear and of tradition. Now those walls were crumbling as they washed one another's feet, and washed their wives' feet.

The white shirts in the front row might have shifted in their seats, but they didn't shut us down. God had his eye on us. He was restraining them. This was His conference.

The following night, we raised the stakes even more. We had an open-air banquet in a city park. This time, there were no restrictions on who could and could not come. No one needed special badges. We were all one in Christ, and we proclaimed that fact in our worship. It was open. It was loud. It was unashamed and utterly unafraid.

We piled into our charter buses after that and traveled to various churches around Havana. There, we held simultaneous worship services all over the city, because this move of fresh unity could not be dependent on foreigners in a tourist's locale. It had to be something they could take ownership of. We wanted the whole church of Havana to experience what we were experiencing—the Kingdom of God as family, the church walking boldly as one.

Did it work? Well, consider what the pastors told me when the conference ended. "We want to start our own alliance!"

It was miraculous. That is precisely how those men describe that week to this day: a miracle. An unmistakable, this-can-only-happen-with-the-Holy-Spirit wonder. And it taught me a profound lesson: you can't rely on precedent when God is leading you, because God isn't bound by precedent. He loves to break molds. He is a divine Pathfinder. Our God revels in blazing trails that have never been blazed before.

So, when I'm seeking guidance and someone tells me, "You can't do that! This has never happened before," I dismiss the concern. It is utterly irrelevant. After all, we serve a God who makes all things new.

Two years later, I traveled back to Cuba. Normally, when I went, I would meet Alejandro and we would laugh until we cried. "Let's party, Jon!" He would say, and we would hit the town and laugh some more. Everywhere he went, "the Billy Graham of Cuba" would meet new people who needed a touch from God. He would pray with them, and the Holy Spirit would show up. It was a thrill ride, with one divine appointment after another.

But this time, there would be no party. I went down because my friend urged me to. He was at home, but he was dying.

"We're not taking any visitors," his wife Alida told me when Ciro and I arrived, "but he wants to see you."

I wasn't ready for what I saw. This was not the exuberant man I knew and loved so much. This was a rack of bones. His skin was translucent and his eyes were sunken. It was clear he had very little time left.

The nurse came in and tried to chase us out, but he was insistent.

"No, no, no!" he said until she relented.

Then, despite his obvious weakness, my friend did something I will never forget.

He climbed to his feet and laid his arms on my shoulders.

"Jon." he whispered in my ear, for a whisper was all he could muster. "Make a covenant with me."

I choked back a tear. "What do you want me to do?"

"You've got to carry on the vision I have for Cuba. Don't stop. Get the Karl Marx Theater." he said.

I knew a little about the Karl Marx Theater. It was the place where Communist leader Fidel Castro had addressed the nation since he took power. From that place, the old dictator would drone on for hours about the glory of the revolution. And his words had taken hold long ago. They had gripped the people. That godless philosophy had held them captive.

"It's been the center of power for decades." Alejandro whispered. "Proclaim God's goodness from that place. And if you do, there will be a tsunami of God's Spirit that will go out all over the Caribbean. Please, Jon. Get the Karl Marx Theater."

It was just like my friend to be thinking of revival on his deathbed. That was the thing that mattered to him more than anything else. He wanted his people to be free of the confines of totalitarianism so they could know Jesus. And it was a perfect request in that it was utterly impossible. The Communist leadership would never open up their most prized venue for a proclamation of the Lordship of Jesus.

So of course, when I heard him say it, I said "Yes, I'll do it. I'll get the Karl Marx. We'll proclaim the name of Jesus from that spot."

"Thank you." he said.

Alejandro died two weeks later. Knowing him—being his friend and serving alongside him—was one of the great joys of my life. And it was an honor to make an impossible covenant with him before he died. After all, we had just seen God part the waters once. We had no doubt He could do it again.

Chapter 15: Nicaragua

"What's next?" That's what we all wondered after the 2004 Havana conference. The whole ordeal had been a thrill ride, and we had all felt it. First Guatemala. Now Cuba.

"Ask of Him, and He shall give you not one, but two nations!"

The answer to "what's next" is almost always a surprise. When God does something amazing, we have a tendency to want to package it so He can do the same thing. But God doesn't work that way. He's not a Divine machine. His ways are often as surprising as they are powerful.

After the dust settled from the conference, we were sure the next big thing would once again involve Cuba. There was talk of hosting a larger, public worship celebration at the Karl Marx Theater in Havana. We loved the idea. But God had something else in store, something we had begun years earlier, something we never saw coming.

Back in the mid-1990s, after the Guatemalan outreach where we visited all those army bases, the generals of that country had continued to gush about how significant our time with them had been. They didn't just talk with one another either, word spread to the generals of a nearby nation.

"We have friends in the Nicaraguan army," a general told me. "And they want you to come there so you can do what you did here with us. Can we set up a meeting with them?"

I wouldn't have known that generals of nations talk to one another on that level, but they had. The Nicaraguan military leaders were eager to see Zion. They were eager to taste the outpouring their neighbors had tasted.

Of course, I said yes. And soon, we had an official invitation from the Nicaraguan army to meet in the capital city of Managua. And so, just months after the Guatemalan campaign ended, I stood before my Oregon congregation and told them about the next outreach location for a Zion team. "We're going to Nicaragua! So get your passports ready!"

Everyone knew the drill by then. Raising up a Zion team wasn't difficult. After what had just taken place with those thirty army bases, people didn't want to miss what happened next. Because in our minds, it was obvious what was going to happen next: we would travel to all the Nicaraguan bases, and thousands would meet Jesus just as thousands had met Jesus in Guatemala. It was clear to us all.

"The officers in Guatemala speak very highly of you," they told me when we arrived at the army base in Managua to set up our drama. "We are excited to see this!"

We were excited, too. Four hundred soldiers came in, sat down, and their commanding officers introduced us. It was all very familiar. Comfortable, even. But something didn't feel quite right. I thought maybe it was just the cold air, but it wasn't. Something felt strange.

Maybe it was the way they received us. The soldiers had collected our passports on the road in, and confiscated our cameras, too. They even seized the camera from our official photographer. None of that had ever happened in Guatemala.

We did the drama just the same as we always did. It wasn't better than average, nor was it worse. It was just Zion. But I could tell right away that these men weren't into it. They sat still and watched, but they weren't buying it. I got up and gave the altar call after that, and some responded, but not many. Certainly not like in Guatemala.

Our Zion team performing

"That was night and day from Guatemala," Ronny said when we left. I agreed. I knew it wasn't going to work. When the general who had invited us called me to say that Zion wouldn't be a good fit for them, I didn't argue. I knew he was correct.

And a voice seemed to say in my heart. "You can't replicate a miracle."

I knew that had to be true. Even Jesus, the ultimate miracle worker, mixed things up when He walked the earth. He healed one blind man with mud, another with saliva, and another with a mere word! (See John 9:1-7; Mark 8:22-25; and Mark 10:46-52.)

If Jesus Himself eschewed predictability, why is it that we,

His followers, gravitate so easily toward formulas? We see God do one thing one way, and we expect Him to do it again, in precisely the same way? It makes no sense.

Something good did come out of that trip, however. We ended up meeting the chief of juvenile police in Nicaragua. His name was Hamyn Guridian.

We had coffee with Hamyn the day after our performance with the army had flopped. We told him about it, and he didn't seem surprised. He told us something like this, "You're not here for the army. You're here for me."

As we struck up a relationship with this man, we discovered he was a wonderful Christian with a big heart. Hamyn was overwhelmed with his job. Gangs were a massive problem in Nicaragua, and the police often felt overwhelmed. After that, we began sending teams to Hamyn and to Nicaragua, but the nation never became a focal point.

As the years passed, the Alliance continued to expand, and we sent teams not only to Central America but to places like Aruba, Romania, India, and China. We were still invested in Hamyn's work, but as far as we were concerned, Nicaragua was just another location.

Then came the Harlem Alliance conference of 2003, and all our attention turned toward Cuba until the next summer in Havana. After that, we expected to be doing more in Cuba. Little did we realize, God was about to place Nicaragua on the center stage.

It happened when we were speaking one day with Hamyn. He was updating us on his work with the youth of Nicaragua, and he was discouraged. Not only was the gang problem worse, he often felt like his own people were against him. It was his police force, after all, that was tasked with arresting kids involved in illicit activity. That put him at odds not only with the gangs themselves but with the parents of the troubled kids.

"So tell me, Hamyn. What do you need?" I asked him.

The answer, I knew, had to be more than simply sending Zion teams down. Evangelism is never the full answer. If we want to affect nations, we tell them about Jesus, but we don't stop there. Every society has broken places that need practical mending. Restoration is the long, hard work of God's kingdom. And here was our friend Hamyn, struggling to build the kingdom in the place assigned to him, but he needed help.

"Really, what can we do?"

His answer surprised us. "Can you get me soccer uniforms?"

Soccer uniforms? That wasn't what I was expecting.

"You see," he said, "we've thought about this. These kids go into gangs because there is nothing else for them. But if we had other options, we could radically curb gang activity."

Nicaragua had soccer leagues, he explained, but those leagues were scarce, and hardly any of them had any funding for equipment. For most kids, then, playing on an actual soccer team was not an option. Uniforms would make the entire dynamic change, he told us. Uniforms would allow for new leagues to begin, new teams to form. It would be a new attractive alternative to the gang scene.

I wondered, though, whether uniforms alone would make that big of a difference. Kids in gangs could still play soccer, after all.

But this was the key to Hamyn's plan. In order to play soccer, the kids would have to make an exchange. In order to be let on a team and receive a uniform, they would have to turn in their colors. They would have to choose between gangs and soccer. It could not be both. Fortunately, as I knew, Nicaraguans love their soccer. I liked the idea.

"How many do you need?" I asked.

His answer was audacious. "Sixty thousand." That response brought to mind the thirty-two thousand bibles in Guatemala. What was it with these massive, unrealistic numbers?

Sixty thousand. I ran the numbers in my head. A good, quality soccer uniform, complete with a jersey, shorts, shin guards and socks, is not cheap. If you looked hard and found a generous supplier, you could get them for fifty dollars apiece. Maybe.

If we found them at that price, they would cost three million dollars. The entire conference in Cuba, including airfare and lodging—the whole bit—had cost us half a million, and that was no small sum. We had to fundraise and pray that money in!

But I had seen too much now to doubt God's ability to come through. Three million dollars wasn't unrealistic. Not really. God had provided those Spanish bibles to us for free, after all, and He could help us get these uniforms, too.

Then I remembered how I had charged forward when General Riviera asked for those Bibles. I had not listened to God but just acted. That had been a big mistake. I didn't want to make it again.

"Speak to me, Lord," I prayed. "Should we say yes to this?"

I knew the answer at once. "Yes."

"Okay, Hamyn. I can get you sixty thousand soccer uniforms." In truth, I had no idea where the money would come from. But God had spoken.

60,000 soccer uniforms ready for shipment to Nicaragua

I shared the vision with the church and with the Alliance members, and we prayed for an answer. Two weeks later, the solution fell into our laps. It happened in Tijuana, Mexico. Ciro was interpreting for a dentist doing ministry down there, and the two of them got to talking one day. Ciro told them all about our soccer uniform dilemma—how we had said yes, but didn't actually have sixty thousand uniforms. The dentist sat up and said, "I know where you can get sixty thousand uniforms in Los Angeles for next to nothing!"

He was talking about a company that specialized in this kind of thing. They had a factory of sorts that would crank out high-quality uniforms for all ages. Their machines stitched and printed shirts, shorts—you name it—in staggering quantities. And sometimes, when the machines would make a mistake, they just kept right on going until someone realized the problem. Thus, they ended up with thousands and thousands of high-quality uniforms that looked fantastic but had very tiny flaws, maybe a stripe in the wrong place, or a stitch that was slightly off. Even though they looked fantastic, the company couldn't sell them.

Ciro told me all about it, and I was intrigued. I called the company and asked them if they had some of those youth soccer uniforms that we could buy cheap.

"Yes, we do. How many are you looking for?"

They were probably expecting me to ask for fifty. Maybe even a hundred or two.

"Sixty thousand," I said, wincing a little.

"Actually," the man said, "yeah, we do. They're sitting here in our warehouse right now." My mouth went dry. I couldn't believe it had been so easy. But there was still the price to negotiate.

"Okay, so how much do you want for them?" The man didn't miss a beat. "If you have twenty-three hundred dollars in cash, I'll let you take them right now."

It was the best twenty-three hundred dollars we'd ever spent. Of course, we had to send them to Nicaragua. We got them all into one shipping container—jerseys, shorts, shin guards, and socks. They came in all sizes so any kid could play. We sent the container down to Hamyn for another paltry twenty-three hundred dollars and jumped on a plane.

Meanwhile, the police put out the word that new soccer leagues were forming. The officers themselves would serve as referees. We saw the response first hand, and it was staggering. Thousands and thousands of kids wanted in right away. I'm not sure what would have happened if the products we sent had looked bad. If they had been low-quality jerseys or ugly shorts and socks, the kids might not have seen the appeal. But the fine materials and bright colors worked their magic. These uniforms looked like the ones the pros wore on television. As such, they represented possibilities that were far more attractive than the ones the gangs offered.

So it happened. The police held huge soccer rallies all around the city. It was a fun, celebratory atmosphere. We even brought a team and performed Zion for the crowds. As kids came to sign up to join a soccer team, they had to turn in their gang colors. They traded their telltale bandanas for a jersey, shorts, socks, and shin guards. The teams formed, and the games started, and the juvenile police force was ecstatic.

There was only one problem.

"Jon," Hamyn told me, "we really underestimated the popularity of these rallies. Everyone wants to join these teams. Can you get me sixty thousand more uniforms?"

When I returned to Oregon, I called the company in Los Angeles.

"I don't suppose you have sixty thousand more soccer uniforms?"

"Yes, we do. And actually," they said, "We might even have

double that. One hundred twenty thousand."

I paused considering the possibility that Hamyn might need more. Was it possible the leagues would really be that popular?

"I'll tell you what," I said. "Let me just buy the sixty for now. Can you hold on to the other sixty? We might want them."

"Sure," they said. And once again, they would only charge twenty-three hundred dollars for sixty thousand uniforms.

So we did the whole thing over again and shipped them down. Hamyn and his team distributed them and started new leagues all over the country. And the kids just kept coming.

"Okay, Jon," Hamyn said on the phone. "Can you send just one more container?"

I smiled. "Yes, Hamyn, we can do that."

And we did.

When all was said and done, we had purchased and helped distribute one hundred eighty thousand high-quality uniforms to the youth of Nicaragua. By our initial estimates, that should have cost around nine million dollars before shipping. We did it for less than fifteen thousand, including shipping.

We knew this kind of effort would impact the nation, but we didn't know how much good it would do. Hamyn reported later that the amount of youth gang activity plummeted. They went from forty youth gangs to just four. Everyone stood up and took notice.

Still, it came as a surprise when the office of the president of Nicaragua, Daniel Ortega, called. They said the president wanted to meet me. He wanted to have a press conference and say thank you for what we had done.

I had a small group of alliance members with me that included my friends Steve Sheer and Ciro. We all got dressed up and went to meet the president. We had to pass through three different security stations before they let us into the large room where the meeting would take place.

Jon meeting President Daniel Ortega

Daniel Ortega was around sixty years old at the time. He had previously served as Nicaraguan president for five years starting in the mid-1980s and had just recently come back into power. He has always been a controversial figure and was known for his disregard for America as a nation and for democracy as an ideal. In fact, Ortega had far more in common with his friend Fidel Castro in Cuba than he did with us.

Maybe that's one reason the cameramen glared at us the way they did. They didn't threaten us outright because they didn't have to. The wires in their ear and the sawed-off shotguns casually half-hidden under their trench coats were threat enough. Those faux cameramen made up only one part of the presidential bodyguard. Men all around the room were heavily armed, and unsmiling.

The press secretary came in to meet us before the president entered. Her instructions were rigid and clear: we were not to shake the president's hand unless he offered his hand first. And we were not, under any circumstances, to approach him or, God forbid, touch him.

But Ortega himself was far more relaxed in his demeanor than the rest of the room was. He walked right up to us, shaking each of our hands in welcome. The "cameramen" didn't like it, but we hadn't broken any rules. He had initiated the handshake, after all.

The press was there, along with actual TV and still cameras. The meeting was being taped for national television, and they would later post it on the Internet, too.

The president asked us to tell our story, and we did. We told him all about the Guatemalan army, and how that spilled over into Nicaragua. We told him about Hamyn's ridiculous request for sixty thousand uniforms. We testified to how it was God that had provided them. Ortega had Communist leanings, but we weren't shy about our faith. We were very open about it.

Then, we pulled out the uniforms themselves and laid them out on tables. He was obviously pleased and impressed. If we didn't know better, we'd have thought he actually liked us. The meeting lasted an hour and a half. It was a warm and friendly conversation, and the president expressed his gratitude for all we had done for his people. Then, he told me this, "You and I have different backgrounds, but we have the same God."

Now, I don't pretend to know how sincere that comment was. I didn't know the man's heart. But I seized upon that opportunity.

"Mr. President, if you don't mind, I'd like to pray for you. Can we pray for you?"

"Yes, you can pray for me," he said. I didn't get up yet. I wanted to be sure he understood.

"Can we get up and come lay hands on you and pray?" Angry glances were being exchanged all around the room, but the president ignored it all.

Praying for Daniel and Rosario Ortega

"Okay," he said. The cameramen were furious now, and my whole team was on edge. But they stood up with me and rounded the table toward the president of Nicaragua.

I turned my head to my friend Steve Sheer and whispered, "Steve, I think you are supposed to pray for the President."

He tried to hide his expression, but I knew what he was thinking. He wanted an excuse to get out of there that instant! But he didn't. We surrounded the president and placed our hands on his shoulders, and Steve began to pray. I didn't look at the faces of the armed guards. We all just closed our eyes and prayed for the president, and maybe for our own safety as well.

The meeting ended without further incident, and we were giddy when we left. We went back to the hotel and waited for the broadcast to air. Just a couple of hours later, we watched ourselves on national television, preaching the good news to the president of an entire country.

And then, the weight of that miracle started to settle in on us. We hadn't done much of anything to make any of this happen. Instead, we had simply listened to God and said yes to His nudging. It was the Holy Spirit who had guided us to the dentist. He gave us favor with the uniform manufacturers. It was He who had turned our path toward a Police Chief over a decade earlier. By listening to and obeying the Lord, we had yet again stumbled into destiny. God had given us another nation. First Guatemala, then Cuba, and now Nicaragua.

God loves to do big things, but He doesn't do reruns. Every miracle is fresh. Every work of the Spirit is unique. His wonders, like His mercies, are new every morning.

Chapter 16: Prison

"I want you to turn Christ's Center over to a younger man." That's what I heard in my heart, and I knew it was God. It had been thirty years since we had begun this ride. In that time, we'd ministered to countless thousands of souls, and ushered masses of people into the Kingdom. We'd made dear friends across the globe and even inherited three nations.

Christ's Center Church was my baby, but I knew it was time to start succession planning. I wanted her to continue to grow long after I was gone, but I knew if she became too synonymous to "Jon Bowers", that would never happen. So I began to ask God who the next man up was.

There were many to choose from. With all our Alliance friends, we had options. But I felt like the Lord said the man was already "in the house." So I began looking around the room even when I was on stage preaching a sermon. And that's when I saw a tall, dark-haired man in his late 20's, dancing in the back of the room. That was him. I knew that was him. My heart sank. The dancing guy? Really? "No, Lord, not him!"

Joshua Rivas had been attending for months, but I didn't know him at all. All I knew was that he worked for a tire company and that he went to my son Ryan's small group.

"What's that Joshua guy like?" I asked Ryan.

"Dad," he said, "he's really the pastor of our small group."

So I called on Joshua one Sunday morning service and asked

if he had a word from God to share with the congregation. And wonder of wonders, he did. It was a good word, too. Full of passion and life. Joshua had little theological training, but it appeared he knew how to hear from God and obey, and to me, that combination was more important than Bible school. Christ's Center wasn't founded on systematic theologies. It was founded on risky obedience.

I invited him and his wife Karen, into my office after that, and I asked him to pray about coming on as my associate pastor. They looked at one another and smiled. It was precisely what God had just spoken to them.

People thought I was crazy at first. The Alliance pastors scratched their heads and said, "What are you doing, Jon?" Many of them even flew in to spend time with Joshua and me. And by the end of those trips, each one would shrug their shoulders and say, "You're right, Jon. I don't know how, but this is God."

Red Crabb and I began to give Joshua some on the job training. It didn't take long to realize he had a real gift with people. He won people over easily and wanted to be everyone's friend. He had vision and zeal, but he also knew how to pastor hearts.

All of that took place in 2007. At the time, I was only thinking about succession planning. I had no idea of the storm that was brewing. I had no notion as to just how much the church would need this man in the coming days. But I would know soon enough.

In less than a year, my life was turned upside down.

My brother and I were told by the government that we had violated the tax code by investing in a trust that we thought was legal. One of President Bush's faith-based initiatives dictated that we could give a percentage of our taxes to faith-based institutions. That's what we thought we had done. Apparently not, they told me. Apparently, we had broken the law.

There is much I could say about the ensuing legal battle, but I have no desire to re-try the case in this book. Suffice it to say, the whole thing started off as a technicality, then escalated into something that still makes no sense to me. There were threats about jail time and whispers about making an example out of us. It got public, and it got ugly. Tensions continued to rise when the local newspaper wrote up a hit-piece on me. People began to distance themselves from me.

Finally, there was a spoken agreement between the lawyers, if we pled guilty to a misdemeanor tax charge, we would pay a fine, and that would be it.

So that's what I did. I pled guilty, but instead of a fine, the judge sentenced me to ten months in federal prison. For a misdemeanor.

I was shell-shocked. Lynna Gay was devastated. My kids were enraged. None of it made any sense.

Those were dark days for us. I know Jesus said, "In this world, you will have trouble," (John 16:33) but this brand of trouble seemed altogether out of step with what God had been doing. Since my heart attack, I had used my talents freely. I had been bold. I had taken risks. I had jumped into the swimming pool even before I saw water. All because God told me to. And He had rewarded my obedience. He had taken us from glory to glory. He had given us nations.

So why this? Why now? God's promises are rich, but His ways are still mysterious. The blessings He gives out aren't always obvious. In the midst of that storm, you're not really thinking about how your suffering might somehow fit into God's plan. All you're thinking about is the pain, the fear, the injustice. All you're thinking about is how your wife will have to go on without you, how your children and grandchildren will have to carry this newfound shame.

And the shame was significant. While my Alliance friends and the elders at Christ's Center stood by me, the local churches around town gave me the cold shoulder. They had read the newspaper reports, and they had believed the gossip. As a result, they didn't want to be associated with me. That stung. I had given my life to the church in the Willamette Valley, and I wished they would call me. They didn't. They had always viewed me as a maverick, now, they saw me as a villain.

Over the weeks leading up to my incarceration, we tried to shut out the noise and make all the preparations we could. I formally passed the torch of Christ's Center leadership to our new pastor, Joshua Rivas. It would be baptism by fire for Joshua. People were leaving the church in droves. He would have to deal with fear, disillusionment, and the church rumor mill. He would have to provide a steady hand and a new way forward.

Finally, the day came. We had prayed a thousand prayers—prayers for protection and vindication, prayers for safety and the nearness of God. There was nothing else to do but embrace the new challenge.

So, in the summer of 2008, I said goodbye to my dear wife and got on a plane headed for federal prison. I arrived at the Federal Medical Center in Rochester, MN—a facility for convicts who had special medical needs. My heart problems necessitated that particular location, which housed medium and maximum-security inmates, and was connected with the Mayo Clinic. I walked through the doors and checked myself in.

"Okay, Lord. Here we go."

The lady at the front desk was incredulous when she saw my paperwork. A misdemeanor? Federal prison was a place for felons! She was so mad, she got on the phone with the office of the judge who had sentenced me and gave him a tongue lashing.

While I waited for the paperwork to be processed, one of the inmates walked by a guard and said something under his breath. The guard responded by clubbing the man over the head. The inmate fell, and the guard dragged him out of the room, leaving a streak of blood behind him.

This was my welcome to prison. Still, I had found favor already. The woman at the desk pulled some strings to get me in an air-conditioned cell with three other inmates. We shared a big window and the luxury of being in a relatively calm area of the facility. Against all odds, I had a nice, quiet room with a view.

The prison was still a prison, however. I spent the first few days trying to figure out what the rules were in order to stay alive. There was always tension between callous inmates and the cruel guards who led them around in chains. It was a vicious place.

But the Lord spoke to me in those first few days. He promised to protect me. I heard the words in my spirit loud and clear: "A chain will never touch your body, and this will become one of the greatest events of your life, one that you'll never forget."

I grabbed ahold of those words and stuffed them into my heart. They were cool water to my spirit. "Lord," I assured Him, "whatever happens, I can assure You, I'll never forget this."

On my second day, I decided to visit the rec room. In our cellblock, there were two rec rooms—one for people who wanted to watch movies, and the other for those who preferred sports. I've always been a sports fan, so I went there. When I opened the door, I saw the room was full. There were probably twenty-five men in there already, and when they heard me, they turned and stared at me. It got uncomfortably quiet.

"This is because you're the new guy," I said to myself and took a quick exit.

A few minutes later, I got a visitor to my cell. He was a large man—probably six foot eight, and well over three hundred pounds. He looked hesitant...almost nervous, even.

"Can I come in?" he asked, knowing that we weren't supposed to let visitors come into our cells.

"Sure," I said.

He had to duck to come inside, and then made his business known straight away. "Did you have to get permission to put paint on your face?"

That wasn't a question I ever expected to be asked. "I don't know what you're talking about," I told him.

But the man was insistent. "The guys in the rec room appointed me to ask how you have silver paint on your face."

"But I don't have paint on my face," I said.

The man grimaced and, without asking for permission, put a swiping finger to my forehead. Then, he inspected his finger. His eyes got big as he looked back and forth from my forehead to his own hand. His face became confused and troubled, and without another word, he ducked out and ran back to the rec room.

The next evening the same man came back and explained, "When you walked into the rec room, your face was shining with silver paint. We had never seen anything like it before. Then when I came in, I saw the paint disappear. I went back and told the guys, and we decided you're either an angel sent to help us, or you're a man of God."

That was how the rumors started. The inmates, having never seen the Holy Spirit in action before, believed I held some secret magic powers. They started coming to me at odd times. They asked me to pray for them in the yard or the weight room or to pray for their sick friends up on the third floor. Soon, I began hearing reports of people getting healed, and the whispers only got louder. Soon, I started to believe what God had told me. Whether or not it was right that I was in prison, God would make something beautiful out of this experience.

The inmates segregated themselves mostly by race. They formed gangs that gave them the protection they felt they needed in that ruthless environment. I didn't want to do that, of course. Instead, I sought out other Christians. They were, coincidentally, the only multi-ethnic group in the place. That in itself was a testimony.

As I got to know them, and the rumors about the silver paint were still fresh, I encountered a mountain of a man I'll call Gabe. He told me the guys had done their homework on me and decided I didn't belong in there. "I'm going to protect you," he said.

He went on to make that announcement to the entire weight room. "This is the pastor. He's a man of God. Anyone who messes with him messes with me!" From that moment on, Gabe became my bodyguard, and nobody messed with either of us.

The small group of believers wasn't very bold, but they were brothers. I met them in the chapel for weekly Bible studies on Thursday afternoons. At first, I told God I didn't want to serve in any sort of leadership capacity. I just wanted to keep my head down. I tried to keep the pastor thing a secret.

That was impossible, though. Not only was the gossip chain already in full effect, but the leader of the Bible study was also already trying to get out of his duties.

"Jon, can you take over the study?" he asked. "If it doesn't go well, you can just shut the whole thing down."

My heart sank. The truth is, I knew I could help. The Bible study had been a disaster thus far. It was poorly attended, boring, and hyper-religious. They needed a fresh start. They needed someone to teach them about the Holy Spirit. But I wanted to stay anonymous.

Fortunately, I had an out. In prison, nobody was allowed to work in his regular profession. If you were a painter in the outside world, you wouldn't be allowed to touch a paintbrush in prison. The guards wanted to keep you uncomfortable and at a disadvantage. Pastors, then, weren't allowed to pastor.

I shook my head. "They won't let me do it."

But the man countered, insisting that since it was an unofficial study, nobody would be intimidated by it. The prison would let it slide.

Thus, I found myself out of excuses. I said yes.

It was on Thursday at two in the afternoon, the single worst time to try to gather anyone. They all wanted to be out in the yard. Four men came, however, and that was enough.

"I want to talk about a man named Gideon," I said, and I proceeded to tell them the tale. It's one of my favorite stories in the Old Testament. Israel is stuck in a cycle of death, suffering, and fear. With no unity, no standing army, and no leadership, they are easy prey for enemies like the Midianites. At the lowest point, those nations are ransacking them with sprawling, pillaging armies. Israel is left defeated and hopeless. In other words, they have a lot in common with the prisoners of the Federal Medical Center. But they aren't alone. God is watching them, and He sends an angel to commission a leader for Israel, someone who could raise an army and fight against the oppressing hordes. He chooses Gideon, a man who was "the least in his family" and his community, and a man so frightened of his enemies that he hid in a winepress while threshing wheat.

When the angel saw this sad display, he did not roll his eyes. Instead, he saw something else. He saw the future God saw. He saw Gideon with heaven's eyes. And when he finally greeted young Gideon, he used these words: "Hail, mighty man of valor! God is with you!" (Judges 6:12)

I applied those words to these inmates. In the eyes of the world, they were castoffs, screw-ups, and dangerous men who would never amount to anything. But God had a different destiny for them. "You might think you're the least in your family and community, but God is saying, "Hail, mighty man of valor!"

I could see they liked the idea, and I asked them to practice using that greeting with one another. So, the four men turned to each other and took turns saying, "Hail, mighty man of valor!"

When they did that, something happened in that room. The presence of God moved in and became thick. I wasn't the only one who felt it, either. The inmates themselves all felt it, and it scared them.

"What the @(*$Y# is happening?" one said, and another man jumped to his feet and said, "I want to get the $*#@(%# out of here."

They left before the bell rang. They didn't know what to make of it.

Naturally, I expected the group would shut down after that. It seemed that God had tried to move, after all, but the men obviously weren't ready for it. When Thursday afternoon rolled back around, however, I found those same four men there waiting for me along with six guests. All ten were eager for the start of the Bible study.

"We told them what happened last time and they didn't believe us," one of them said, referring to the new men, "so we brought them with us this time. Can you make that happen again?"

I smiled. "I didn't do that. It was God. I can't make any of that happen. But I would like to teach about Gideon again since these gentlemen haven't heard it yet."

So I told them the exact same story and gave them the same challenge. They turned to each other and said it, "Hail, mighty man of valor!"

And once again, the Holy Spirit fell. The environment changed. The presence of God brought a warm, disarming atmosphere. I watched and waited. The six newbies were hardened men, but they were feeling it, too. The men who invited them grew excited.

"See? We told you! He has magic powers!"

"No, I don't have powers," I said. "This is God doing this. He wants to let you feel His presence to show you how valuable you are. And that presence you feel right now can be with you all the time, in your cells. It can be with you even when you go to the hole."

"How do we make that happen?" They asked. And I showed them Romans 10. "...If you confess with your mouth the Lord Jesus and believe in your heart that God has raised Him from the dead, you will be saved."

All ten of them were saved that afternoon. They all wanted to meet Jesus. They all wanted His Spirit to go with them wherever they went.

They were hungry after that. Even after the bell rang, they wanted me to keep on teaching them about Jesus, but I had to shut the meeting down. I told them we would re-convene the next week.

The following Thursday, the group went from ten to twenty men, and the group was eager to hear me tell the story of Gideon.

Before long, the words of the angel to Gideon became a rallying cry inside the prison. You could hear the call from one side of the cellblock to the other. Men would be walking down the center aisle, and people would call to him, "Hail, mighty man of valor!"

They reveled in the phrase. Something resonated inside them when they heard it. Some of them knew what it was, and some didn't. I did, though. I was beginning to see what the Lord meant when He promised to use me in this dark and desolate place. He had given me a message for a place that was full of Gideons. The Holy Spirit saw them, He was for them, and He still had plans to give them a future and a hope. And who knows? Maybe I needed to hear that message just as much as they did.

Chapter 17: The Rev

"What's this mighty man of valor thing all about?"

That was the question swirling around the prison. The phase signaled a change in the atmosphere. As people began to get saved, they also began to experience encouragement and joy, and that joy spread.

I was beginning to feel a surge of excitement and faith with all of this. Sure, the prison was mostly awful. Who wants to live locked in a cell where everything you do is dictated to you, where you have guards breathing down your neck, and where a wrong look can land you in the middle of a gang war?

But then, I had been in the middle of scary environments before. I had ministered in war zones. I had been interrogated in Communist strongholds. I had stood before a president who hated my country, and whose bodyguards wanted to nail me to the wall.

What if I treated prison the same way? What if this was just my next adventure, where God would do amazing things? God was already following through on His promise to protect me, and He was already showing up.

So I began to take on that posture. The past was no longer important. It didn't matter why I was there anymore. The trial, the injustice of it all… I had to let that go. I had to embrace the present. I was on a mission's trip.

That's when it got fun.

As the weeks went by and the Bible study continued to grow, I asked the chaplain if I could have a recording of the Zion play sent to him. When it came, I asked if we could show it for a church service on Sunday. He gave me permission, and soon, the entire place was abuzz with the news that something unique was going to happen on Sunday.

There were usually around twenty men that would come to a church service, but on that Sunday, there were more than two hundred. My heart swelled.

They all took a seat, and I told them what they were about to see. Then I hit play on the VCR and sat down with them while they watched the recording. If I could have brought in a live drama team, I would have. In fact, I decided right then and there that when I got out, I would bring a Zion team to the prison so these men could get the full effect but for now, a videotape would have to do.

But screen or no screen, the men could feel the truth in what they were watching. The gospel message, even when recorded on a crummy videotape, still packs a punch.

At the end of the drama, I stood up and gave my customary invitation for the crowd to receive Jesus—to trade in their soiled hearts for a new one, white as snow. I told them it didn't matter what they had done. God saw them and all their deeds, He saw their darkened hearts, and He wanted to give them a new beginning. He was ready to forgive anyone.

The response was overwhelming. Almost every man in there prayed to receive Christ. I invited them forward to get a symbol of their decision, a white handkerchief. The church back in Oregon had sent me a box of them, and I had to get permission to give them away. The men formed a line, and the guys from the Bible study handed them out one by one.

It was a powerful moment to see these hardened men turn their hearts over to the Lord. My helpers felt it, too. There was a surge of joy in the room, and in heaven. The angels were partying, and we all knew it.

"Jon, We're going to run out of hankies," my helper said.

"That's okay," I told him. "Just keep handing them out until they're gone." I watched him as he did it, and his eyes started to widen.

"This is freaky, Jon," he said. I keep getting to the bottom of the pile, but every time I lift one up, there's another one right beneath it!"

On and on the hankies went. As long as men stepped up to receive one, there was always one more beneath it. We did the math later on. We gave out twenty more hankies then we started with. That might sound unbelievable to you, but that's fine with me. I was there, and I know what I saw. And let me tell you, there are no small miracles in prison.

After that day, the inmates stopped using my name and started calling me "The Rev." They used the term without a hint of irony. It was their way of honoring me, and it made me terribly uncomfortable.

"Lord, what do I do with this?"

"Just accept it," He seemed to say. "I see your heart. I see you're doing it for me. Let them call you what they wish."

Weeks and months went by. God's Spirit was so active now. I was praying with people all the time. Salvation was breaking out all over the place.

One Friday afternoon, a man I'll call Collin came to see me in his wheelchair. We had met before in one of the Gideon bible studies. Collin was a veteran of prison life. He had been behind bars for nearly fifty years. Most of those years had been at the infamous Fort Leavenworth, but they transferred him to the Rochester facility because of a terrible growth he had on his foot. It was like a huge knot on the side of his big toe. Believe me, it was nasty, and it required surgery. He always wore a stocking to hide its ugliness.

"Rev, do you really believe that stuff you said last night about God forgiving anybody?"

"I sure do, Collin," I answered.

"Well, I can prove you wrong," he shot back. "I'm the worst sinner here, and nobody can forgive me. Do you want to hear what I did?"

"Sure, if you'd like to tell me." For the next half hour, I listened to Collin's confession. It was a story unlike any I had ever heard.

At seventeen years old, Collin was already done with life. He wanted to kill himself, but he couldn't make himself go through with it. Instead, he concocted a plan: he would rob a bank, get caught in the act, and force a guard to gun him down. For some reason, that sounded easier to him than shooting himself. When he put his plan into action, he took a revolver along with him, which he never intended to use. He thought it would encourage the guard to shoot him. But after he had stolen the money and the guard approached, Collin panicked. He pulled out the gun, shot the guard dead instead, then fled the scene in his pickup.

Nobody caught him. Nobody was even chasing him. Somehow, he had successfully robbed a bank and gotten away with it. So, he decided to try again by robbing another bank. This time, he thought, he would undoubtedly be killed. But once again, nobody shot at him and nobody apprehended him. And once again, he killed someone else in the process.

Five times he did that, and each time the result was the same, Collin was still alive with more money in his pocket, and at least one more person was dead. As the body count climbed, reports of Collin's crime spree spread all over the news. He had stolen more than twenty-five hundred dollars each time—a lot of money back then—and it was becoming an exciting game for him. So Collin decided to up the stakes. He got his hands on some putty and nitroglycerine to make a makeshift bomb. He stuck it on the back of an armored truck, lit the fuse, and ran. He thought the explosion itself might kill him. And indeed, it killed some. The boom was awe-inspiring, shattering windows up and down the block. Dead and wounded bystanders lay all over the place, and money was raining from the sky.

Collin, half-dazed and numb to the suffering he caused, ignored the screams and entered that wreckage. He pulled out several bags of money, threw them in his truck, and sped away without anyone stopping him. No guards, no cops, nothing. He thought he was dreaming. It was all so easy.

By then, he had amassed a small fortune, and a new thought began to occur to him. Rather than continuing to pursue his own death, he could just take his money and disappear. He could retire on some island somewhere and live out his days in comfort.

But before he did that, he decided to rob just one more bank. This time, however, they caught him, and the jig was up.

All of that had happened forty-nine years earlier. The Collin who sat across from me was sixty-six years old. He had spent his entire adult life paying for those crimes, and his time in prison had not been good to him. In truth, he was a mean, hardened man. And he wore his hardness like a cape.

"So tell me," he said after he finished his story. "You honestly think your God could forgive someone like me?"

I looked him in the eye. "Collin, I'm telling you this not because it's my opinion but because the word of God says it. God loves you, He sent His son to die for you, and if you accept Him, you can receive salvation and forgiveness."

Our conversation went elsewhere after that, but the seed had been planted, and it wouldn't take long to germinate. In fact, Collin came to me the very next day. He wanted to repent. He wanted to ask God's forgiveness. He wanted to ask Jesus to save His soul. I was only too happy to help him do it.

That encounter would have been miraculous if that's all that happened, but it wasn't. God had more for this man. He began mingling with the other Christians in the cellblock.

Sometime that week, he joined me at my card table in the rec room and asked to be my partner. We started playing, and sometime in the middle of the game, I felt God speaking to me in a most unexpected way, "I want to heal Collin's toe." I looked around. There were probably forty other guys in the room that day, and I knew if I initiated a prayer for healing, they would start their jeers. Still, I knew I couldn't disobey.

"Collin, I think God wants to heal your toe," I told him.

The response came at once, "Rev wants to pray for Collin's toe!" they howled. I was a respected prisoner by then, but they couldn't miss an opportunity to unleash unfiltered, obscene prison humor.

I didn't care, though. I took his stocking off and pulled Collin's foot onto my knee. Then, my roommate Cal and I prayed aloud that God would heal his toe. It was a simple prayer, and when I was done; he put his sock back on and wheeled himself out of the room.

The next morning, as we got up, I walked out into the corridor, looked down the hall, and there was Collin. He wasn't in his wheelchair. Instead, he was walking on his own two feet, and he was coming toward me.

"Rev! Rev! Come here! Come look at my toe!"

We stopped at a couple of plastic chairs, and he whipped off his stocking before I had a chance to say anything. And the growth was just...gone!

The doctors confirmed the news when they saw it, his foot was healed. I'm sure they didn't chalk it up to divine intervention, but they saw the result. Somehow, that growth had completely disappeared overnight.

"There's only one problem," Collin told me. "Now I'll have to go back to Leavenworth!"

Word of that healing spread like wildfire throughout the prison. The entire prison—more than 900 inmates and guards—all heard the story of Collin's toe. For those who were close to the situation, there was no denying what had happened: the Rev had prayed, and a miracle had come.

Even the guards began to change the way they treated me. One day, I was going to meet my wife in the visitation room. A guard was there to escort me.

"You mind if I call you Rev?" he said to me.

"Why would you want to call me Rev?" I asked, somewhat surprised.

"Because that's what you're known by in this prison." He said. I could see he wasn't making light of the nickname. His eyes were earnest. So I asked him what I could do for him, and this is what he said:

"I'm watching what you're doing in this prison, and I want to receive Jesus Christ, or whatever it is you do to get people saved." I prayed with him right then and there.

After that, we began having favor with the guards. I even gained permission to go pray for people on the third floor where the hospice patients lay in their beds, waiting to die. These patients received regular visits from a sweet little nun who would deliver soda and small gifts to try to lift their spirits. When she first invited me to come with her, I said I had no desire to deliver pop. If I was going to visit dying inmates, I wanted to pray with them. She agreed to let me do that, and I brought salvation cards with me.

That day, we visited eight inmates. All of them were near death, and they knew it, too. One of them was a skeleton of a man whose eyes got big as we approached.

"This is the man they call the Rev, the nurse said to him.

"You're the Rev?" He asked, getting excited. "Oh, we know all about you up here! Will you pray for me?"

"I can do better than that," I said, holding up the card. "I can give you a ticket to heaven!" He burst into a smile at that and said. "I've been asking everybody how to get to heaven, and nobody knew!" I led him to Jesus right there at his bedside. You'd be hard pressed to find a happier convert. He died the next week.

It went on like that. One patient after another received Jesus. Only one patient wouldn't let me pray for him. Seven did. Seven men accepted Jesus as their Savior for the first time. None of them lived long after that. They were all eleventh-hour conversions.

At the end of the night, I asked the nun why she had been delivering soda. Why hadn't she been praying with the inmates like we just did?

"We're not allowed," she said.

I shook my head. "Don't believe that. You are anointed of God to bring the good news to these men. You have everything you need."

She got emotional. "If I do that I'll lose my job. They're watching everything we do," she said, pointing to the cameras. "And they're already planning on moving you out of here. But if you send other inmates from your Bible study, they can pray with these men after you go."

I found out later she was right about their plans to move me out. The only reason they didn't is because they thought it would incite violence from my cellblock. The guys had grown protective of me, and they would have been furious if the guards took me out for no reason.

But I liked her idea of passing the torch, and that became our strategy. I began to focus more on discipling the inmates who had gotten saved. I wanted them to not only receive the grace of Jesus for their sins but to extend that grace to others. I wanted them to become soul winners, too. And they were.

The best example of this is a man I'll call Russell who had recently met the Lord in our Bible study. One day, Russell came into our study looking forlorn and emotional. He told us his dad died.

Familial deaths are always hard in prison. The regrets are always as thick as the desire to be there for the funeral, but that never happens. Russell told us, through his tears, how he had been the black sheep of the family, how he had let his father down. He wanted to go to the funeral, which was only an hour away from the prison.

So even though there was almost no chance that he could go, we prayed that he would gain permission. Sure enough, the Lord heard our prayer.

Russell could attend the funeral, but he would have to go in the company of two armed guards. He would have to wear his orange jumpsuit, too, and would be chained the entire time. But he didn't want to go empty-handed. He wanted to bring salvation cards. He wanted to show his family how Jesus had forgiven him and saved his soul. And best of all, he wanted to give them the same opportunity.

Of course, the guards wouldn't allow him to bring such contraband, so we hid thin stacks of cards all over his person. This was not a time for rules. This man was on a mission, and we wanted to help him.

The church was crowded with mourners that day, and Russell had to make the walk of shame all the way down the aisle to the front row with his accompanying guards. There he sat in his prison clothes—the bad seed in his family. The great disappointment. He had to endure all of those stares while watching the service and saying goodbye to his father.

At the end, he raised his hand and asked if he could say a few words. The pastor graciously said yes.

So there's our man Russell, standing before the congregation. He asked for help taking off his shoes. In his sock was hidden a stack of salvation cards that the guards had somehow missed. And there, in front of all the friends and family who had been so ashamed of him, Russell preached the gospel. He told the crowd that He had met Jesus and that Jesus had forgiven him his sins. And if they asked him into their hearts, he said Jesus would forgive them, too.

Then the convict-preacher gave an altar call, and many prayed to receive Jesus as their Savior.

When he came back to us, he was elated by all that God had done on his behalf. I knew that feeling well. Indeed, I wanted them all to know the feeling of God's favor. In fact, that was the premise for the feast that was soon to come.

When Christmas rolled around, I had a talk with my roommate, Cal. He had become my primary disciple in prison—a dear friend and a partner of the gospel.

"I want to have a Christmas feast," I told him.

It was a ridiculous idea, of course. Nobody threw feasts in prison. The guards would never allow it. But by this time, ridiculous ideas were my favorite kind of ideas. What good was an idea if you didn't have anything to risk?

So Cal agreed in spite of himself, and we started to make our plans. We pulled a bunch of the guys together, and all agreed that we would begin to buy food from the prison store and stockpile it for the appointed day.

Of course, in prison, we were pretty limited in what we could buy. There were sodas and cookies and cans of tuna and shrimp. There was popcorn and chips and moon pies. It doesn't sound like much, I know, but when you've been in prison for a long time, these treats are small delicacies like manna from heaven.

For weeks, we went quietly about our little plan. We bought the food with our own money and divided up the loot in various cells. None of it was against the rules, and none of it was even secret, per se. The guards were always watching, and we knew that.

Still, we were fairly certain they didn't exactly know about the feast, either. They hadn't put two and two together.

As we drew close to the big day, I had a talk with one of the guards. I told him we were going to have a party, and I wanted it to be special. I wanted to use the big basins the officers always used for all their cold drinks. And I wanted to use the fancy plates the officers ate off of.

"You know I can't do that," he said, rolling his eyes.

But I was bold. "Sir, I want it here for the big day."

He hesitated a little. "Look, I'm not even going to be working on Christmas Day!"

At that point, I knew I had him. "That's okay," I sad. "Put them in the storage closet. They've already given me that key for my kitchen duties."

He sighed. "Look, it's not gonna happen. God bless you guys, but I can't help."

That should have deflated me, but it didn't. There was something about the look on his face.

"Cal, he's going to do it," I said. "He's going to get us those dishes." When Christmas came, I opened the storage closet and glory! The guard had put the dishes in there, along with everything else I requested.

I got my crew together, and we began to set up tables and retrieve all the food we've saved up. We got the whole rec room looking beautiful, and set the food out in a spread these guys hadn't seen in years.

Word began to spread, "There's a Christmas party at noon. Everyone in the cell block is invited!" Of course, the prison guards were all finding out now, too.

"They're going to shut this down," they said. "The warden is on her way."

Nevertheless, we carried on.

The plan was not just to throw a party; it was to throw a

banquet. This wouldn't be a regular prison meal where the men came through the line and grabbed the food with their hands. Instead, they would come through with their nice dishes, and we would be there with the blue gloves the janitors wore. We would serve them. Prison, after all, is a place where dignity comes and dies. We wanted to revive it. These men were created in the image of God. I could tell them that all day long, but they needed more. They needed to feel it.

Finally, we heard the warden's chains jingling as she came down the corridor. She burst into the room, looked around, and raged.

"Who's responsible for this?" There were about fifteen of us in the room. We had still been busy putting butcher paper on the tables, setting the food on platters and soda cans in basins. All of us stopped and looked at one another.

Then, one of my guys answered: "I'm responsible."

Before I could protest, another one spoke up. "No, I'm responsible."

Then, a third. "No, I'm responsible." All of us claimed full culpability for the Christmas feast that day. It was a real-life Spartacus moment that made me both thankful and proud.

The warden, however, was not amused. She abandoned her question and demanded to see receipts for all this food. Cal sprang into action. "I've got them right here." he said. And I knew it would all check out. We had been meticulous about saving receipts.

She looked at them, then spat out one more threat. "I'm going to check this out and come back. I assure you, this party is not happening." She stormed away, never to come back. We had won the day.

When the twelve o'clock hour struck, all the men from our cellblock flooded into that room, and we had a feast, unlike anything they'd ever seen. The men walked through the line where we greeted and served them. They were mighty men of valor, after all.

They sat down and ate a delicious Christmas meal together—something many of them had never experienced in their entire lives.

After we ate together, it got quiet as we read the Christmas story aloud, and I told them all about Jesus, who loved them so much He came to earth to give His life on their behalf. I gave an invitation to know this Jesus, and many more men responded. It was one of the most beautiful meals I've ever experienced.

That feast felt like the culmination of what God had done in prison. I still had time left to serve, but the end was in sight and I knew I had done well. I had treated the men with love and had introduced hundreds to Jesus Christ. The same Spirit that raised Christ from the dead was transforming the lives of these criminals—these men were precious sons of God.

Indeed the entire atmosphere was changing. Fights were way down, unity and encouragement were way up. It was like in the book of Acts 19:20, where "the Spirit of God was triumphing mightily." That was never more apparent than it was that Christmas Day.

Yes, I could have ridden off into the sunset after that. But there was one more challenge that came to me. One more risk to take. This time, I was not eager to grab hold of it. It happened when I had just three weeks left before my scheduled release. We were having our Bible study when one of the guys we didn't see much came busting in to interrupt us. His friend was in hospice care up on the third floor, he said, and he was dying.

"Rev, he's going to hell. We've got to go get him saved!" And yes, that was undoubtedly true. This man's friend had helped to run one of the largest drug cartels in the country.

There was no way I could go up there, though. It was not visitation time, and nobody was allowed up there without very special permission. In fact, there was a sign outside the elevator that said any unauthorized person caught up on that floor would be arrested (yes, you can get arrested again in prison) and prosecuted immediately. In other words, he would be sent to the hole and would be in big trouble. His sentence could be extended. Things would not go well with him.

But I only had three weeks left on my sentence. I was about to go home!

"Oh, God," I said in my heart. "Please send someone else up there, someone from the Bible study. Anybody but me!"

But He spoke firmly to my heart. He said, "Trust me. This is just the kind of thing the apostles went through."

"But Lord," I countered, "the apostles were also thrown into the inner dungeon."

"Yes," He said. "But they survived. My Spirit will be with you. Go." I was so scared that my knees were literally shaking beneath me. Finally, I pulled myself up out of my cot and said to the man, "Come on, let's go."

Cal tried to stop me. He told me I would be thrown in the hole, and that they wouldn't release me back to my wife. But I was more bullheaded than he was, I was not about to back down.

"Fine," he said. "But if you go, I'm going, too." The three of us ventured up to the elevator. We had less than ten minutes before all the doors would be locked, and we'd be left outside.

"Okay, here we go, guys," I said as we stepped into the empty elevator. The door closed, and we pushed the button to the third floor."

There was a guard station right next to the elevator, so we had to slip out quietly and head straight to the dying man's room. Somehow, we made it. We saw at once the man's eyes were closed, and his face was weak. You could tell just by looking at him that he didn't have much time.

"Here is the Rev," the friend told him. "He has your ticket to heaven!"

The patient's eyes opened at those words, and he looked at me with a hopeful smile.

"Okay," I told the dying man. "Your friend here is going to lead you to the Lord. Go ahead."

The friend hesitated. "I can't remember the prayer," he said. So I whispered the words into the friend's ear, and he led the dying man in the sinner's prayer. In a moment, they were holding one another, weeping sad and joyful tears. Then, I felt a hand on my back, and I knew we were caught. When I turned around, however, I saw the face of another inmate with tears in his eyes.

"Can you do that for me, too? I'm dying, and I'm going to hell!" So of course, we prayed with him, too, and he received Jesus.

As soon as we prayed with that second man, we had to run to the elevator to get back inside. Once again, we would have to slip past the guard station.

This time, however, we didn't make it.

The guard was furious. He read us our rights and shoved us back into the elevator. I'm not sure I've ever seen a man so angry, he was raging at us all the way down to the bottom floor.

Now by this point, I figured it didn't matter anymore. I could be as bold as I wanted to be. I was already in trouble, after all. So I opened my mouth and said the thing I really wanted to say. "You shouldn't be angry. That man is going to heaven. You're not. You're going to hell. But you still shouldn't be angry because you could go to heaven if you'd just accept Jesus."

That comment was gasoline on his fire. I knew it would be. His face turned red, and he unleashed a spectacular string of curse words. A vein was popping out of his neck.

The elevator stopped at the first floor, and we all stepped out. Well, almost all of us: me, the cartel friend who had brought us up there, and Cal. But that was all. Somehow, inexplicably, the guard stayed in the elevator. Even while he was still screaming, the door closed, and the elevator went back up to the third floor.

We stood there, shell-shocked. He was gone. We were sure he would return in a moment, but he didn't. All we could do was try to go back to our cellblock, except there was nobody to let us in. Then, out of nowhere, a woman came—a guard we had never seen before. She asked what we were doing there, and we told her plainly all we had just done on the third floor.

"That's the most beautiful thing I've ever heard," she gushed at the story of the two men's salvation. Then she asked where we needed to go. We told her, and she picked up her radio and said this:

"Cellblock one-two, I have three gentlemen here who are just completing some work for me. I'm sending them back."

It was like a dream. The doors opened, and we all returned to our cells. The guard never came for us, and we never heard a whisper about any of it.

"Who was that woman?" I asked the other men. They had both been there longer than I was, but they swore they had never seen her before. I knew I hadn't. And to this day, I sometimes wonder whether she was a divine messenger, sent to keep us safe. After all, hadn't God promised me His protection?

Three weeks later, on the heels of that miracle, I was released from the Federal Medical Center. My lovely wife met me at the door, and we wept for joy at the goodness of God. A chain had never touched my body. No one had ever laid a finger on me. No harm had come to me, even in the midst of that dark place.

Indeed, that dark place was home to the greatest season of ministry I've ever experienced. It was greater even than my time in Guatemala, Nicaragua, and Cuba. Indeed, it was the best missions trip I've ever been on. And there are some days, I confess, that I miss my home in prison.

Chapter 18: The Karl Marx Theater—God did it!

It's been ten years since I walked out of federal prison. Ten years and a thousand switchbacks up the mountain as God led me. Many things have changed in that time. I left Oregon in 2011. I left because Joshua had the church well in hand. I felt the time was right to say goodbye to my home state. So, I followed my son Ryan to Texas and started a new season of life.

Karl Marx Theater

The Dallas Metroplex couldn't be more different than Junction City, Oregon, but I love it still. I love my new church—Gateway Church, one of the largest and most active congregations in the country. I love every big and little thing that I've been blessed with. All of my children and grandchildren live near us, and we have fallen in love with North Texas. Since I'm not pastoring, I don't have much official work to tie me down. That means I can focus on my grandkids and continue mission work around the world. Life is good.

I was going to end this book with those updates. God’s written a new chapter for Lynna Gay and I, including a different home and a new rhythm of life. We’d embraced it all. But there was one thing missing—the Karl Marx Theater. The covenant I had made with Alejandro. He had been gone for a long time now, and I hadn’t made any real progress in fulfilling my promise. That still irked me. Covenants are weighty things. When we make a covenant, I think the angels shush each other and bend their ears. They remember.

Alejandro’s widow remembered, too. Alida is a strong woman, one of the strongest I've ever known. When her husband died, she took the reins of the church and made it grow. It's become one of the largest in the country, with hundreds of church plants spanning the breadth of the island. Every time I visited Cuba, Pastor Alida would take my hands in hers, and we would both begin to cry about the covenant. We both remembered. We both waited.

But despite my best efforts, I couldn't seem to make it happen. What else could I do but put it in God's hands? I prayed, "God, you gave us Cuba once. Give us Cuba again." And that’s how I was going to end this book—in faith that God would hear my prayer someday. A promise made, but not yet attained. That’s okay. Like the heroes of the faith in Hebrews 11, they didn’t all attain the fullness of the promise either. But God would be faithful. He would follow through on His word.

For now, though, I had done all I could do. I had made so many trips to Cuba that I lost count! The government's tactics remained as frustrating as they were the day Ciro, and I first stepped into Castro's compound. They gave evasive answers and half commitments. They canceled meetings without warning. They told me, "No, no, no! You're never getting the Karl Marx Theater!

And then, all of a sudden, they said, "Yes." Which means I get to end this book the way I always wanted to.

It happened because of a man named Victor, who was in charge of popular music and cultural events in Cuba. He had been the one at the top of the pyramid for years, throwing up roadblocks for us at every turn. He had not been an ally.

But on one trip in the spring of 2019, something changed. Victor's people had decided to take our side. He had three main officials working under him who had all decided to vouch for us. That in itself was a small miracle. Somehow, we had won them over with our vision.

So, one afternoon, when I was about to go to see a play at the Karl Marx, we got a phone call from Victor, telling us to stay put because he was coming to meet us personally at the hotel. My contact, a Christian artist named Juan, was stunned when he got the call. This was not normal. This was big. So, we stayed right there and waited in the lobby of the Melia Cohiba hotel.

Victor was thick with hefty shoulders, dark skin, and large glasses. I could tell at once he was a severe man."Mr. Bowers," he said when we sat down. "I have religious groups from all over the world who want to do events at the Karl Marx Theater. Big names and big acts from all over the world. I've said no to every single one of them." His implication was clear, but he went on to spell it out for me anyway, just in case I was too dense to understand.

"Mr. Bowers, you are a nobody!" He pointed his finger in my face. It was an aggressive gesture that irritated me.

“Well, you realize I’m talking about bringing in world-class musicians for this," I said. "It's a gospel concert. I won't be on the stage." That was a newer strategy we had taken. Instead of seeking to preach a sermon from the stage, we decided to preach through song. God works through the arts at a deep level. Deeper than through spoken words, sometimes. Plus, this kind of event would fit in well with Cuba’s dedication to jazz music. I had so many relationships with churches and a diverse array of wonderful musicians. I knew it wouldn't be hard to pull an event together. It had obvious appeal. Not only does Cuba love music, but the Cuban government also loves a good photo op.

Victor shook his head. “Still, no one knows who you are. Why would I ever let you do this?” I asked him if he had done his research on me. Had he heard of the conference we had fifteen years ago in the very hotel that we were sitting in at that moment?

"Sure," he said. “But you're still a nobody." And here's the tricky thing—he was right. I had worked very hard to keep a low profile. Despite all that God did throughout the decades, no one had any idea who I was. I had kept my head down. I had remained a nobody.

That's why I answered him the way I did. "Sir, maybe that's the reason you'll let me in here. Maybe it's because I'm a nobody." At that, Victor stopped and gaped at me. He hadn't expected that. A smile spread across his face.

"Mr. Bowers, I like you. I think you and I will be friends.” And he gave us the Karl Marx, just like that. We signed the contract. Three nights. Three shows. I was stunned. So many years of waiting, and then it happens in a flash.

I got on the phone right away. I called Carl Phipps, Mel Holder, and Michelle Sweeting from Harlem—three of the finest gospel recording artists in New York. I called Tyrone Jones in Yuma. I called my own pastors at Gateway church in Dallas. I told them to bring their worship teams, because we were going to

Havana for three-night gospel concert at the Karl Marx Theater—something that had never happened in the history of this nation. God would finally be praised from the center of communist power!

Everyone signed on. I didn't have to twist anyone's arm. They could sense the truth—God had prepared all the ingredients for us to make history.

Fifteen summers after our first conference in Cuba... fourteen summers after I made my covenant with my dear friend, Alejandro... ten summers after I left federal prison, I returned to Havana with forty-one of my most adventurous friends.

It was September 11, 2019.

We gathered in a jazz cafe, all forty-two of us, along with a couple of dozen Cuban musicians and technical staff. It was a fancy restaurant made for tourists. There were neon lights on the wall, a disco ball on the ceiling, and massive windows facing the Avenida de Maceo seawall across the street, where waves struck and smothered the sidewalk in white foam over and over again.

I held the microphone, and I told them the story. Not all of them had heard about Alejandro, and my promise to him. Not all of them had heard about his faith, or the faith of his widow, Alida. And very few of them understood what a holy moment we were entering into. We were standing on a hill build of prayers. For decades, Cuban believers have battered heaven with this request—that God would be glorified in Cuba. That He would be lifted above all other powers.

We worshipped openly that night with hands raised high, and voices lifted higher. We prayed that Jesus—the center of our joy—would be glorified through our efforts. And we thanked Him for the privilege of letting us be involved in His business.

Then, we celebrated with dinner and a concert. A Cuban jazz band wowed us. Their fingers flew over keys and strings with such ease. Such optimism. For half an hour, they held us all spellbound. That kind of freedom—that irrepressible joy—is what these people were made for. They were made for improvisation. They were made for a wild, adventurous God who has big plans for them—plans for a future and a hope.

From the beginning, I knew I wanted to include that spirit in our concert. I wanted Cuban musicians to play a big role. Music is woven into their culture in such a beautiful way. It's a part of who they are. On any given night, the streets of Old Havana teem with exceptionally talented guitarists, horn players, and drummers. There are always drums of some sort, inspiring everyone who hears them to dance.

That same joy shines through in their Sunday worship services. Alida's church alone features some world-class musicians, and they had agreed to join us. Now I had them all in one place: Cubans, Texans, New Yorkers, and Arizonans. It was a dream team!

Two nights later, we gathered in the green room behind the stage at the Karl Marx. This was the room where Castro and his friends would convene before and after their events. The room was bugged, I was sure, but I didn't care. They knew what I was about. We had already prayed openly in that room. The day of rehearsal, we sang a capella songs of praise in English and in Spanish. Beauty echoed from every wall.

The mood changed when Victor suddenly came into the room. Victor, the man in charge. Victor, the man who had put his finger in my face to remind me that I was a nobody.

When I saw him, he hardly looked like the same man. His countenance was so different. He was smiling like the proud host of a great feast. "Hello, my friend," he said, opening his arms.

I wanted to roll my eyes and say, "Oh, give me a break! You put this thing off for years!" But I realized there was no harm in letting him play the hero. He asked if he could address the team.

Everyone listened to him quietly. He said he admired them for being brave. It was a courageous thing for Americans to come to Cuba in the middle of such political turmoil.

He was right about the tension. Things had been rough between our two nations over the past year. The new economic embargo had made life in Cuba particularly difficult. The country was hurting financially. There was a major oil shortage, which was wreaking havoc on the economy. Shops all over the city were shutting down at noon, and the buses weren't running. We expected the lack of public transportation to limit the size of the crowd that night.

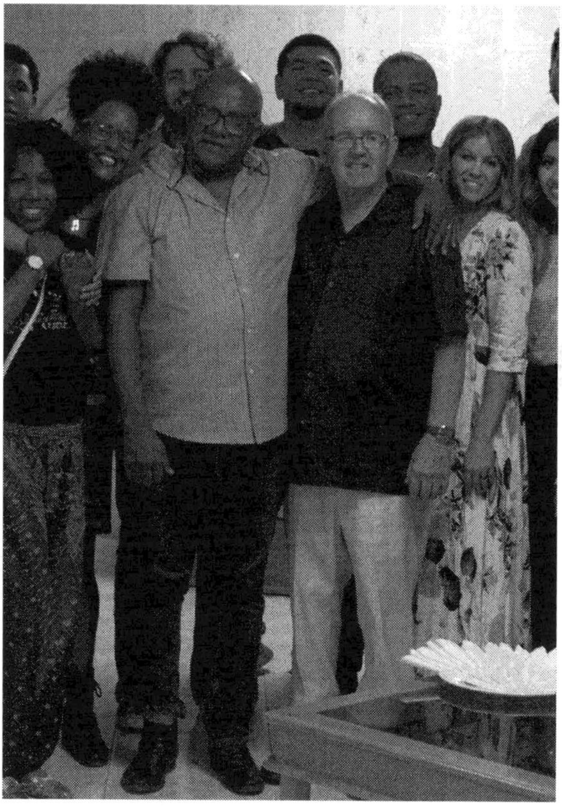

Victor and Jon

Victor went on, “But you made a good decision to unite your music with our music. If there's one thing that was never broken between us, it’s the music. We have that in common!”

We all applauded him as he left. The concept of a cultural exchange was truly what had made this happen. Different tribes, tongues and skin tones would join together to lift the name of Jesus in the common language of melody and harmony—that had been a primary feature in all our old Alliance trips. It was at the center of this one, too. It was as if God wanted to remind us that unity and beauty go hand in hand.

When Victor was gone, some of our team asked about seeing Alida. I shook my head. “There’s a chance she’ll be here tonight, but she won’t be able to talk to us.” I said. “It’s been a really difficult time for her. The police have kept her under close surveillance, and it’s too risky for her to make contact with us.”

In truth, it was worse than that. The Church's relationship with the government had been even more strained than usual. In recent months, two of her pastor friends had been arrested, and she had been detained and interrogated.

So no, we probably wouldn’t see Alida, I explained. Then I turned around and saw her—the living picture of confident grace. She wore a beautiful black evening gown because this was a special night. A covenant was about to be fulfilled.

"I had to come," she told me. “The other pastors are afraid. They think this is a trap. They think they'll all get arrested. I have to prove to them that it’s safe.”

This surprised me. Many of the pastors had been with us in 2004. They knew me and trusted me. But this time, they were afraid the government had duped me. Once the theater was full of people, they thought the police would bolt the doors and arrest them all by the thousands.

But here was Alida, offering herself up for her people as a sacrificial lamb. The courage of this woman made me shake my head in wonder. Her leadership was so bold. What an example of faith! She had a regal bearing, and it was all to honor Him.

"Tomorrow, I'll call them and tell them it's safe. And I figure if they do arrest me tonight, well, at least I'll get arrested with my friend!" We laughed and embraced each other, two travelers who had endured a long, hard journey.

The theater itself is relatively plain by American standards. It is towering, with two balconies and roughly six thousand red cushioned seats. The walls are barren except for some light fixtures and exposed wiring. The plain decor doesn't do justice to the outrageous history that flows from there.

The Karl Marx Theater is the nation's premier public venue, but it's more than a concert hall. Much more. It is the epicenter of power for Cuba. Many of the biggest political and cultural edicts have come from that place. When a popular band flies in from Europe, they go to the Karl Marx. Likewise, when their president wants to speak to the nation, he packs the theater, fires up the TV cameras, and takes center stage.

Jon and Alida

I had been inside the theater a couple of times when it was empty. I had climbed the massive wooden stage and walked to the small metal square where Castro himself used to stand for his three-hour rants. “Jesus, be glorified from this spot!” I had prayed.

And finally, sitting in the audience, I could feel the expectation. We all could. We could feel it as everyone filed in on Friday night, then Saturday, then Sunday. Something was happening in the invisible realm.

The curtain opened with Mel Holder, on the saxophone, Ithiel Torres on the trumpet, and Carl Phipps on the piano playing "How Great Thou Art," because that's what Alejandro had wanted all along. That song was dear to him, and he wanted that declaration to be the initial focus of attention when the night finally came. And boy was it! When Michelle Sweeting strolled on stage with her microphone and began belting out the verses, the crowd rose and sang with her, their arms lifted in praise. They didn’t notice what I noticed—Michelle was standing and jumping on that metal square.

The diversity of the performers was impossible to miss. Our New York contingent was made up of African Americans, and our Arizona team, City Lights, was mostly Latino. My friend Tyrone Jones, one of the Alliance pastors, brought the worship team from his church. When the emcees introduced them, they launched into the modern praise anthem, "Raise A Hallelujah." The lyrics couldn’t have been timelier:

I'm gonna sing, in the middle of the storm

Louder and louder, you're gonna hear my praises roar

Up from the ashes, hope will arise

Death is defeated, the King is alive!

There were only around eight hundred people that first night. Fear of arrest, along with the lack of buses, hindered the turnout. But it didn't restrain the enthusiasm of the Cubans in that theater. They were on their feet, letting their praises roar. Hope was rising!

More people came on the second night. On the third night, the entire lower level was packed out. Over four thousand worshippers crowded in. That's because the pastors were able to repeat Alida's message to the people—this was no trap. This was the real deal. An actual worship service on hallowed government ground.

"I've lived my whole life here, and I've never been in this theater," Alida had told me, looking up at the rafters. "I've never been allowed." That made me think of a dear Cuban pastor friend, who years before had driven us there so we could walk around the theater and pray discreetly. He was so nervous about it that he parked his van two blocks from the place. Even being near that building drew the eye of the police. And here we were inside it, singing in the middle of the storm.

There were two massive projector screens on either side of the stage with the words, Arte Y Amor. Art and Love. That's what government officials had called the concert, and it was a night of art and love. During each song, the media crew displayed moving graphics to go with the music. We saw images of the cross, and of the empty tomb, pictures of chains breaking. In the Karl Marx Theater, chains were breaking. I wept at the realization.

A Cuban a capella quartet performed. One of their wives was backstage. She told my translator that she and her husband had performed all over Cuba, even on television, but any time they sang about the Lord, the cameras would be turned off. The woman shook her head in amazement. She never thought it could happen in Cuba, least of all this place—crowds singing openly in Spanish and English, praising God with arms waving.

"You don't know what this means to us," she said. For most of the ninety minutes, the crowd was its feet, worshiping in wonder, and capturing the history on their phones. When I slipped out to the restroom, there was a woman attendant at the door, which is common. She didn't see me coming at first. She was crying with her face in her hands.

"Are you okay?" I asked her, and she jumped. I had startled her. "I'm sorry. Yes, I'm okay. It's just," and she motioned toward the music. "It's just so beautiful!"

As we watched the concert, Alida sat next to Lynna Gay and me. Around us sat many of our dear friends who had spent years praying with me to see this victory come to pass. We were all emotional. How could we not be?

The Gateway Worship team closed out the evening. They sang in English and Spanish, and they blew the roof off the place. By the time they reached the final chorus, everyone was standing, and all of the night's performers were crowded onstage, belting out these words in two languages:

Your promise still stands

Great is Your faithfulness, your faithfulness

I'm still in Your hands

This is my confidence, You've never failed me yet!

And I think this song is the perfect summation for my whole unbelievable story—how I heard God on a tractor, and how His promises led me on this unlikely adventure spanning the globe. Through church splits and civil wars, through prison cells and the revered halls of dictators, the message has always been the same—His promises stand.

This is why I keep going. I'm well into my seventies now, but

I'm not backing down. I want to use all of my talents, not just three. Because the fact is, only God is worthy of the sacrifice of my life.

When He calls us to do the impossible, He is faithful to create miracles. We can trust Him with everything that concerns us. Sometimes His miracles come like a sudden Texas thunderstorm. Sometimes they come slowly and gently, like a soft rain in the Willamette Valley. Either way, He will be true to His word. I should know. He's never failed me yet.

He won't fail you, either. You don't have to be a hotshot pastor or a seminary graduate to build His kingdom. You don't need vast resources and you don't have to have fame. You can be a nobody like me. All you need to do listen to His voice, trust His word and have a willing heart.

I heard His voice back in 1973 on the 806 International Tractor. For these past decades, I've had to buckle up and hold on tight, because He's taken me for a ride. My ride isn't over, even after this adventure. In fact, the concert went so well that Victor has thrown open the doors for us to do even more. He wants us to come back and play again at the Karl Marx and beyond. We've played in the most prestigious hall in all of Cuba and as a result, we are free to go to any other venue. He even said we could play at the amphitheater, which seats more than sixty thousand people.

To that I say, "Praaaaaise God!" That's one step closer to our goal of seeing open air evangelism in Havana. We want the Cuban Church to be released, to be able share her faith without fear. To be as strong and as free as she was meant to be.

It will happen. I know it will. Because I've watched Him do the impossible.

History was made at the Karl Marx

The grand finale at the Karl Marx Theater went on for more than ten minutes. Our Latino worship leader, Jacobo, took command of the stage, praying bold prayers for the nation. As he launched back into the chorus of the worship song, thousands of voices rang out and the curtain slowly dropped:

I've seen You move, come move the mountains

And I believe, I'll see You do it again!

You made a way, where there was no way

And I believe, I'll see You do it again!

Amen

Jon and Lynna Gay Bowers, Kim Mills, husband Levi, with—Erika, Anthony, Aiden, Eli, Evelyn Brandon, Marci, Gavin, Raegan, Todd Bowers, wife Jamie, with —Sydney, Jordan, Cooper, Spencer, Claire, Ryan Bowers, wife Crissie, with—Justice, Paige, Trent

An Invitation...

Do you know Jesus? You can pray this simple prayer to become a Christian.

Father God, I confess that I am a sinner and I repent of my sins. Jesus, I believe that you are the Christ the Son of the living God. Today I accept you as my personal Lord and Savior. Thank you for saving my soul.

"If you confess with your mouth the Lord Jesus and believe in your heart that God has raised Him from the dead, you will be saved. For with the heart one believes unto righteousness, and with the mouth, confession is made unto salvation. For the scripture says, whoever believes on Him will not be put to shame. For there is no distinction between Jew and Greek, for the same Lord over all is rich to all who call upon him. For whoever calls on the name of the Lord shall be saved. Romans 10:9-13

If you have accepted Jesus, please contact us at iheard806@gmail.com . It would be our pleasure to connect you with a church in your area so you can fellowship with other believers and grow in your walk with God.

Made in the USA
Columbia, SC
11 February 2021

32790483R00113